PAIRFECTION

PAIRFECTION

MARK HURST

PLAIN SIGHT PUBLISHING
AN IMPRINT OF CEDAR FORT, INC.
SPRINGVILLE, UTAH

ISBN 13: 978-1-4621-1480-1

Published by Plain Sight Publishing, an imprint of Cedar Fort, Inc.
2373 W. 700 S., Springville, UT 84663

Distributed by Cedar Fort, Inc., www.cedarfort.com

LIBRARY OF CONGRESS CATALOGING-IN-PUBLICATION DATA

Hurst, Mark W., 1951- author.

Pairfection : a quirky look at marriage / Mark W. Hurst.

pages cm

Summary: Discusses how perfect marriages do not exist. Addresses the marriage/mirage relationship in a unique, visual, and creative way.

ISBN 978-1-4621-1480-1

1. Marriage. 2. Marriage--Religious aspects--Church of Jesus Christ of Latter-day Saints. I. Title.

HQ734.H95 2014

306.81--dc 3

2014006905

Cover and page design by Angela D. Baxter

Edited by Daniel Friend

Printed in the United States of America

10 9 8 7 6 5 4 3 2 1

Printed on acid-free paper

DEDICATION

TO JILL, WHO PUT UP WITH 40 YEARS OF IMPERFECTION

CONTENTS

INTRODUCTION

I'M A WRITER, OF SORTS. I want to start out by telling you that. This is a book about marriage, and I want to get the fact that I'm not an expert on marriage out of the way. I'm not a counselor. I'm not a sociologist. I've never studied marriage or family relationships, and I'm not an expert on any of it.

I'm a writer.

I've spent most of my adult life in the business of advertising and marketing. Yes, we write clever jingles and taglines. I've written and produced hundreds of ads for television, radio, newspapers, magazines, and billboards, as well as digital messaging on the web and for social media.

Our industry is not, however, just about clever slogans. If it helps you to think of us that way, OK. In a larger sense, we try, in our profession, to understand customers—what moves them and what they care about. When we create strategies for our clients, we focus on aligning their product or service with the real needs of the people who will use it.

We try to measure what they **KNOW, THINK, SEE, FEEL, AND DO,** and we try to find ways to talk to them about what really matters. In a book on marriage, we should focus on all the things we should know, think, see, feel, and do in a marriage.

Throughout the years in my profession, I have leaned on an important concept to help understand and develop a great customer experience. It's called a *needs/wants quotient*. There are products people need (Crest toothpaste) and products people want (Harley Davidson motorcycles). When we attack a marketplace, we focus on what people think they need and convert it into a want, a longing. If people want something bad enough, they make it a priority on their own. We simply nudge them in that direction.

That's why, in the world of marketing communications, we have to be creative. This is another word for *sneaky*. We help consumers feel that their wants are actually needs—things they can't live without.

Recently, I've been helping complex technology companies find their place in a crowded market. I write integrated marketing communications strategies to help them succeed. Modern technology changes virtually weekly and monthly, and messaging consultants have to help these companies understand that they can't sell their products on features alone. They need to help their customers make a deep commitment to a brand, to the way it solves problems, and to the way it makes an enduring connection with human emotions and the way humans live their lives.

That sounds like marriage—deep commitments, solving problems, enduring connections to the deepest of human emotions, and understanding needs and wants.

INTRODUCTION

Advertising isn't rocket science, but it is my profession. When people ask me what I do, I tell them I'm a writer. It's a lot of research and head-scratching, and it's a lot of creative thinking and planning. Then you write it all down.

And all the creative types in the advertising world believe that they have a screenplay or a book inside of them and that if we could just find the time, we would write our manuscript and become famous. We all see ourselves as writers.

This book isn't like that. I had no desire or interest in writing a book on marriage. It just sort of happened. But I've had a cluster of thoughts in my head about the needs/wants quotient of people who practice and work really hard at this thing called marriage. What is it? How does it work?

So I decided to write about it.

But it's not a traditional book. You could read it cover to cover, or you may want to browse it, use it, and refer to it occasionally, finding sections that help you out. There might be a thought or a moment here and there where your marriage will benefit from a simple minute or two of scrutiny.

You see, marriage is like a lot of those technology companies I work for—a lot like the way we position them in the marketplace.

MARRIAGE IS A FLUID, DYNAMIC, AND EVER-CHANGING UNDERTAKING. WE HAVE TO BE DEEPLY COMMITTED TO IT, TO SOLVING THE PROBLEMS AND CONFLICTS THAT ARISE, AND TO THE WAY THAT MARRIAGE MAKES AN ENDURING CONNECTION WITH HUMAN EMOTIONS.

MARK HURST

INTRODUCTION

We have to have a clear understanding of the needs/wants quotients of the players in a marriage: one man and one woman.

It begins with this idea: there is no such thing as a perfect marriage. I can't write about the perfect marriage and list the steps you take to get there because **PERFECT MARRIAGES** ARE **PERFECT MIRAGES.** They don't exist. Notice how close those two words are: *marriage* and *mirage*. (Hopefully your marriage is more than a mirage.)

All around the world, people struggle with the word *perfect*. We talk a lot about it. People of the Christian faith are taught that this life is about coming to earth, receiving a physical body, and learning how to emulate a perfect, deified being—Jesus Christ. It's his tough injunction to "Be ye therefore perfect" (Matthew 5:48)—the impossible goal. The unreachable dream. It's sometimes even a silly notion, considering what flawed people we are. Yet it's the heart and essence of Christianity.

> "IF YOU LOOK FOR PERFECTION, YOU'LL NEVER BE CONTENT."
>
> LEO TOLSTOY

"BE YE THEREFORE PERFECT."

Isn't there something else? "Be pretty good. Be ye therefore mediocre."

Speaking of advertising taglines, why don't we use the one from the razor company Gillette: "The best a man can get." Let's use that as our motto instead of this whole perfection thing. Let's lower our standards and try really hard to simply be the best we can be. Wouldn't that be OK?

"I AM CAREFUL NOT TO CONFUSE EXCELLENCE WITH PERFECTION. EXCELLENCE I CAN REACH FOR; PERFECTION IS GOD'S BUSINESS."

MICHAEL J. FOX

Only one person was perfect, according to the scriptures, and that was Christ. In him we have a partner with God. He intercedes with God and helps us get back into heaven—back into an eternal life in God's presence.

INTRODUCTION

"TO SAY THAT ONE WAITS A LIFETIME FOR HIS SOUL MATE TO COME AROUND IS A PARADOX. PEOPLE EVENTUALLY GET SICK OF WAITING, TAKE A CHANCE ON SOMEONE, AND BY THE ART OF COMMITMENT BECOME SOUL MATES, WHICH TAKES A LIFETIME TO PERFECT."

CRISS JAMI

Here's what I think it means: Reach for perfection. Strive for perfection. Be like Christ. Be humble, be meek, be submissive. Be forgiving, loving, longing, caring, giving, genuine, and gentle. Be honest with others and true to yourself. It is the quest for Christ-like living that, day by day, leads us through the

PROCESS OF **PERFECTING.**

SO THERE YOU HAVE IT: PERFECTION IS A PROCESS.

GUESS WHAT? SO IS MARRIAGE.

Religious leader Lorenzo Snow talked of marriage and family unity saying the scary words "be perfect." But here's the whole quote:

> Should there not be union in the family? . . . Most assuredly there should. And why should any man be satisfied, why should any husband and father of a family rest satisfied until he effects a perfect union, that is, just as far as a perfect union can be accomplished? [Husband and wife should be] prepared to make their children just as perfect as they are willing and capable of being made perfect.[1]

I love it. Let's put in huge type: **"AS FAR AS A PERFECT UNION CAN BE ACCOMPLISHED."**

And the best part of his thought? Don't rest. Keep trying, keep working, and never be satisfied.

THIS IS A BOOK ON MARRIAGE, NOT RELIGION.

I'M A LATTER-DAY SAINT. I try to be a good one. I'm very, very, very imperfect, but I'm doing the best I can with what meager assets God gives me. I've wanted to draw on all of my life experiences as well as my church service to talk about marriage and what Elvis Presley called a "crazy little thing called love."

You're already starting to see that it isn't going to be only about the scriptures but rather about a lot of other things designed to help you think about marriage, focus on your relationship, and put into the routine or your life. It will include little mnemonic devices to help you remember that you're working on it and doing the best you can. In advertising and marketing, these devices are clever taglines, catchy jingles, little stories, and slice-of-life scenarios.

As I said, taglines do very little to sell you products, but they help connect you, in simplest of terms, to your needs/wants quotient.

INTRODUCTION

For many years, the General Electric tagline was "We bring good things to life." I like it a lot. It doesn't say that GE makes lightbulbs or toasters. They make large jet engines, huge wind turbines, CAT scan machines, and a lot of other phenomenal products and services—including lightbulbs—and they summarize all the ways they make life better for the human race in one catchy line. You're not going to buy many wind turbines or CAT scan machines, but I bet you have a pretty good impression of GE and their products. After all, they bring good things to life.

This is a good platform for the rest of the book:

MARRIAGE:

IT BRINGS GOOD THINGS TO LIFE.

The book is designed with both words and pictures. It's graphic in the way an ad guy would do it, so it's easy to scan, easy to remember, and easy to connect with. It's meant to be fun, not serious and preachy. It's written to make you comfortable with striving for a good marriage instead of the folly of a perfect marriage. Did I mention that there's no such thing?

Individually you can't be perfect, so it's pretty safe to say there is no such thing as a perfect marriage. It can't happen, so stop trying.

I might occasionally tell you about my marriage—a little story here and there to give my thoughts context. My marriage certainly isn't perfect—far from it!—and I'm pretty sure that every marriage, like every fingerprint or DNA strand, is very different. Each can be very successful in thousands of different and unique ways. So there isn't a road map or a floor plan or a play-by-play handbook. At least, I've never seen one.

I knew a couple once who always seemed to fight. I actually asked the husband about it, and he said, "Fighting? We never fight. We confront and then move on. Never confuse fighting with loudness.

We're simply loud. That's how we make sure the other one is listening."

I had wrongly judged his marriage, and I decided then to never judge another. I have close friends and family members who have struggled with marriage and have dealt with divorce. It's never a good thing, and it always seems like there should be some way to fix a broken marriage or save it before it falls apart.

Or start out differently.

There are no formulas. There is no magic. Don't listen to anyone who tells you they have the answers. Run from those who claim to have the rules, the secrets, and the code for growing, healing, building, creating, or nurturing a marriage.

We all do it differently. Half the fun is making it up as you go along. (I'm not sure what the other half is.)

This not an indictment or even a criticism of marriage counselors or psychologists or clergy. They may be very helpful for certain individuals or couples who occasionally get stuck. I hope so, anyway.

I'm just not sure that there is a textbook formula to follow the way some people think there is or the way we sometimes think there ought to be. I'm pretty sure there's no crystal ball. I've never seen it.

Ready for another ad slogan? When I got married and was nervous about it, I sought out some advice from trusted friends. I worried that I couldn't afford it. I was still attending university and had a really bad job and wondered how it all works—paying rent, buying food, and not having parents as a backstop.

One particularly bright fellow said this: "If you wait until you can afford it, you'll never get married." I've told lots of young people the same thing. You can't afford to wait.

I wasn't sure I was emotionally ready for marriage either. And I suppose the same advice is true. If you wait until you think you have all the skills for marriage, you'll never get married. Don't wait. Believe the Nike tagline and "Just Do It."

THE 40-YEAR EXPERIMENT

AGAIN, I'M NO EXPERT ON MARRIAGE. I've never pretended to be, and I won't start now. I've been an ecclesiastical leader in my church, and such leaders are often called upon to give counsel and advice, and we have to rely less on books and training and more on common sense, wisdom, and the promptings of the Holy Spirit. Sometimes we are called upon on as untrained amateurs to solve big-league problems. We all do the best we can to help each other understand the intricacies and the nuances of the marriage experiment.

The only expertise I have on the subject of marriage is somehow, fortunately, doing it for 40 years. On exactly the date of my 40th anniversary to a woman who is beautiful inside and out, I sat down and wrote this book because I wondered two things: First, how did we do it? A number of people in our circle of family, friends, and work colleagues wanted to know. Second, I know how I've made it with her—she's great. What I genuinely wanted to know was this: how did she put up with me?

My wife's name is Jill. When she and I celebrated 40 years, I bought her 40 roses. I was proud as a peacock, she was touched, and it was such a tender, intimate moment that there was only one thing to do: post it on Facebook for our combined 1,200 or so friends.

I got a lot of pats on the back for the roses: "Way to go, dude." Jill got a lot of compliments: "What a lucky girl." And a lot of people asked us for advice. Lots of people asked how we did it. So I thought about it and wondered if I knew how we did it. If so, was it worth sharing?

I don't want to tell you how we did it. I don't want to give advice. But it did make me think about a lot of things, so I started a list. I'm going to give you those thoughts, pretty much as a list, and you can decide which of the items might be appropriate for you and your spouse/partner.

I can't tell you how to have a great marriage. I can't tell you how to have a long, enduring marriage. I can't tell you how to have a happy marriage. I can tell you that all three are possible. And I can tell you, with all certainty, that it's worth the effort.

"IF THERE IS SUCH A THING AS A GOOD MARRIAGE, IT IS BECAUSE IT RESEMBLES FRIENDSHIP RATHER THAN LOVE."

MICHEL DE MONTAIGNE

WHERE IS THE MARRIAGE HANDBOOK?

THERE ARE NO RULES. There certainly isn't a how-to handbook. With **MARRIAGE** we do it by **DOING** it. We **ENDURE** by **ENDURING.** Happiness is the result of overcoming hardship and pain and making sure we are engaged in the pursuit of happiness. That word, *pursuit*, means going after it, digging, working, searching, scraping, clawing, and sweating for the right way to do things. The Disney Corporation has tried to convince us for years that their theme parks are the "Happiest Place on Earth." And for moments in time, with children in tow, we escape the mundane meanderings of life and enter a fantasy world where mice talk and princesses rule. Our goal is to make marriage the happiest place on earth. When we do, we get very, very close to heaven.

INTRODUCTION

We don't **FIND** happiness. It doesn't find us. We **MAKE** happiness possible by the way we put ourselves in a position to recognize it, embrace it, internalize it, and demonstrate our willingness to live it. There is no such thing as a lifetime of happiness. There are only

MOMENTS OF HAPPINESS

and contentment and peace and fulfillment and deep emotional connection that we gather together into a bundle like a bunch of freshly cut daisies. This collection of grand moments results in a bouquet of happiness. True happiness is a grand collection of small moments of great delight.

Marriage is the concept of striving for perfection—emphasis on *striving*. It is on-the-job training and it takes a lot of time, effort, commitment, and hard work. And acceptance that it won't always be magical. (You do realize that mice can't talk, right?)

Back in the '70s, 40 years ago, when society was filled with hippies, free love, campus sit-ins, riots broken up with tear gas and bullets, a culture in turmoil, and a world seemingly turned upside down, what did a couple of young, goofy kids married in their early twenties do to survive the chaos, noise, near poverty, grinding, groaning, and the overall gut-wrenching experience we call marriage?

Like the song from *The Sound of Music*, let's start at the very beginning. That's a pretty good place to start.

"I HAVE LEARNED THAT ONLY TWO THINGS ARE NECESSARY TO KEEP ONE'S WIFE HAPPY. FIRST, LET HER THINK SHE'S HAVING HER OWN WAY. AND SECOND, LET HER HAVE IT."

LYNDON B. JOHNSON

IT STARTS WITH LOVE

LET'S ASSUME IT STARTS WITH LOVE.

Probably. Most relationships start with lust. And that is as natural as a peacock spreading its feathers or any other beast strutting their stuff and emitting pheromones. We are physical creatures, programmed to primp and posture and pine and strut; built to lust, drool, pant, sweat, shiver, shake, and flat-out lose our minds over a pretty girl or a hot guy. We are physical creatures compelled by physical drives.

It's easy to fall in lust. It's a little more difficult to fall in love.

Don't tell me what's pretty in a woman. That's up to you. Don't tell me the physical features you're looking for in a man. I don't care. It's a personal interpretation. Spoiler alert: you're never going to get a perfect-looking spouse. If your search is focused on looks alone, you are already destined for failure.

LOOKS FADE.

CHINS SAG. BELLIES BULGE. SKIN WRINKLES. LUST *DOESN'T* LAST. LOOKS *DON'T* LINGER. YOU HAVE TO LOOK BEYOND LOOKS AND LIVE BEYOND LUST.

I spoke earlier of features and benefits in a product or service. Humans look at other humans and examine their features. That's where we start: pretty faces, long legs, flat abs, curves or lack of them; square jaws, broad shoulders, blue eyes, red hair, dimples, curls, and straight teeth. And then we pass judgment on them and decide whether or not features are acceptable or attractive, or if we can live with a few warts and less-than-perfect complexions. We put physical features into our needs/wants quotient.

Then we settle. We compromise. Finally, we forgive. And when we forgive, we are able to look deeper. And it's when we go deeper that we find gold. Temperament, personality, emotion, tenderness, consideration, responsibility, accountability, devotion, faithfulness, understanding, and responsiveness all trump pretty or handsome. And they last much, much longer.

It's easy to fall in love. That's an interesting word, *fall*. It's also easy to fall off a cliff. Falling is fine if you're willing and able to pick yourself up and nurse the bruises and the skinned knees. But generally speaking, falling is not a good thing. Falling is fraught with peril. It's much better to stroll into love, lean into love, mosey into love, and evolve into a love where your feelings, passions, longings, lusts begin to align with the lasting qualities of harmony, peace, contentment, compatibility, and joy.

INTRODUCTION

If it's an action verb you want, don't *fall* in love; find someone who makes you jump for joy. *Leap* toward love.

Now, in the spirit of transparency, I'll tell you something. I'm going to be honest. And I'm going to be honest because if I don't tell the true story, my wife will, and I'll be shown a fraud. (She does that so well.)

I've just issued a bit of a caution about falling in love. The fact is, I fell in love. I fell hard. My wife and I were both at the University of Utah, and a friend set us up. It was a blind date to a Roberta Flack concert. This female vocalist got very famous with a song called "Killing Me Softly." Jill killed me softly that night. By the end of the concert we were in love, four weeks later we were engaged, and five months later we were married.

Following our first date, we were never apart and never dated anyone else. Was it dumb? Was it dangerous to fall that hard? Forty years later, it seems stoically touching. I've been in a position to counsel young couples, and I think that kind of speed is horribly dangerous, even though it worked for me. I was very much in lust with an attractive young woman, and I'm grateful that the concept of evolving into deep love worked its magic on us.

Conversely, we have friends who dated for six years before they knew they were in love and had the courage to get married. They too just celebrated 40 years. Six years for them, six hours for us. Go figure.

There is no perfect marriage, there is no perfect courtship, and there is no perfect path to love and marriage. There is only the quest for perfection, and your pathway is probably the right one. Your approach is as good as anyone else's.

"A SUCCESSFUL MARRIAGE REQUIRES FALLING IN LOVE MANY TIMES, ALWAYS WITH THE SAME PERSON."

MIGNON MCLAUGHLIN

BEING PAIRFECT

SO, IN THE WAY KING ARTHUR spoke to Merlin the Magician, let's start this way: "Proposition: there is no such thing as a perfect marriage." You won't have a perfect spouse—there's no such thing. And you'll never have a perfect marriage. It is an impossible ideal.

But, with some work and focus, you might be able to have a **PAIRFECT** marriage.

You would expect an ad guy to invent a new word. What does it mean to be *PAIRFECT*?

First, marriage is a pairing—two people coming together to form a new whole that's better than the sum of its parts. It's a coupling, a linking, a binding, a bonding, and a sealing. There's even the biblical admonition to become "one flesh."

At the end of two arms, we have a pair of hands. Most of the time they work together. If we are right-handed, the tasks of life like writing, eating, and swinging a baseball bat are done with our dominant hand. But most of the time it takes a pair of hands to open a jar, type a story, comb a child's hair, make a sandwich, drive a car, put on clothes, applaud a great performance, ride a horse, fell a tree, swing a child, or signal a touchdown. When things get too tough or too busy, we say, "I could really use an extra pair of hands right now."

When it's cold outside, we buy a pair of gloves. Or, on our feet, we wear a pair of socks. (Hopefully they match.)

Interestingly, we also wear a *pair* of jeans or a *pair* of pants. One definition of *pair* is: "an article or object consisting of two joined or corresponding parts not used separately." Jeans don't really come in pairs—you buy jeans. You buy pants. They have two legs hooked together, making them corresponding parts not used separately.

The Wrangler jeans company currently tells us their jeans have more room in the butt and that their product is "real, comfortable and right."

I think marriage is a really good pair of jeans. It's a pair of corresponding parts not used separately. And a good marriage is real, comfortable, and right.

Second, as I started writing down my thoughts on 40 years, believing that there must be something interesting along the way, I started with a list of words, including the word *pair*. It jumped out at me and it helped me invent the word PAIRFECT. As I compiled that list of words, there were two that didn't have a completely natural feel with the rest, but the list seemed incomplete without them. In fact, they are the essence of everything else I'm trying to say here. Those two words are *authenticity* and *integrity*. (You'll read about them a bit later.) The first letters of those two words, *a* and *i*, placed inside the word *perfect*, changed the spelling to PAIRFECT.

When I did this, it changed everything. I knew I couldn't talk about perfection—I'm too fundamentally flawed. Most people are flawed. Most marriages are flawed. So many marriages are imperfect.

I needed a different word.

I knew I couldn't write about a perfect marriage because there is no such thing. I knew I couldn't write about my marriage and its 40 years of survival—what worked for me may not work at all for you.

I knew I couldn't simply gather a collection of what others think a perfect marriage is because we've probably already heard most of that, and it would be their formula. It's what worked for them.

AND SO, THE NEW WORD PAIRFECTION

Another reason for this new concept is the word **AIR** right in the middle. Marriages occasionally will need air—oxygen—to breathe. Catch your breath. Take a breather from one another.

Occasionally in marriage, you need to blow things up—like habits, sameness, mundaneness, ruts, and rigidity. Get some air underneath the marriage.

Elevate it. Lift it. Let is soar.

DRUDGERY IS THE **ENEMY** OF A **GOOD MARRIAGE.** DAILY GRIND, DUTY, AND DEMANDS ARE **NO SUBSTITUTE** FOR **ENERGY, ELEVATION, EXCAVATION, AND ELATION.** **GET UP, GET OUT, GET GOING.** GO, DO, LIVE, BE, WONDER, WANDER.

That's sort of what the book is about—finding ways to catch your breath and put a little air under the wings of your partnership. With that in mind, let's begin our quest for **PAIRFECTION.**

IT AIN'T EASY BEING ME

VIRTUALLY ANYONE I'VE TALKED TO agrees that marriage is hard. It's really, really, really, really hard. Changing from "me" to "we" just because a preacher says it's so is really quite impossible and mostly preposterous. Changing from "I-centered" living to the plural "we" is a big jump and a bit unnatural. Romantic? Yes. Easy? Not a chance.

I like the idea of growing everyday.

CHANGING. CHASING. BETTERING. IMPROVING. BELIEVING THAT BETTER IS ACHIEVABLE.

STRIVING FOR THE REACHABLE, COMPLETELY COMPREHENSIBLE IDEA AND THE REALLY TENDER ADAGE OF LOVERS EVERYWHERE: "I AM BETTER WHEN I AM WITH YOU."

"I am better because of you." "I am more of me when we are more of we."

When there is "more of we," selfishness goes out the window and selflessness flies in. *We* means *team* and *teamwork*.

MARRIAGE is the not the act of SAYING I DO, but of DOING.

On certain days, the concept of "till death do us part" feels like "this is going to be the death of me." Giving of oneself for another and giving up oneself for the benefit of the "we" is brutally complicated and complex.

Achieving perfection is impossible, but achieving PAIRFECTION one little step at a time may well be in your grasp. Here's a list, kind of like ingredients on a recipe card, for achieving PAIRFECTION. You can tweak the ingredients a little if you like, and you may have a few of your own that the rest of us haven't discovered yet. Did I mention that there are no rules?

P

is for PERSISTENCE

WHAT A GREAT FIRST WORD to have on our list. Persist. Keep going. Hang in there. Believe that it will work. Believe that you are a good spouse—you are. Believe you are a good parent—you can be.

Winston Churchill, rallying his nation in a time of war, said, "Never, never, never, never give in." He was speaking of freedom and the commitment to liberty. In marriage, repeat it four times: "Never, never, never, never give in." Never give up on a marriage that can and will work with persistence.

> "CHARACTER CONSISTS OF WHAT YOU DO ON THE THIRD AND FOURTH TRIES."
>
> JAMES A. MICHENER

P *is for . . .*

At a Sunday dinner just a few weeks into our new marriage experiment, we entertained guests. This was the menu: Roast beef, mashed potatoes, dark brown gravy, and broccoli. Here's what we ate: a rubber fishing boot, wallpaper paste, roofing tar, and broccoli. (The broccoli was very good.)

Forty years later, we entertained about 20 family members one recent Sunday. The menu was crab-stuffed mushrooms, jalapeño-crusted baby back ribs, caprese salad with basil fresh from our garden, roasted corn on the cob, and raspberry cheesecake. What we ate was a five-star, restaurant-quality feast. Our early attempts at cooking were disasters. Now we cook and take cooking classes together, and we are getting really good.

Symbolically and realistically, there are going to be a lot of burnt roasts in your marriage—but also some really tender steaks.

It took a lot of time to learn about other things—like sex, cooperation, and sharing and integrating cultures and values. We failed a lot of times at a lot of different things, but now we can barely remember them. We celebrate the successes.

Early sex was about lust and passion and hurrying up and making babies. Lots of nights lacked romance. Later, it became tender, slow, moving, satisfying, warm, deep, and meaningful. First attempts were awkward and one-sided. With persistence and patience, it became mutual and balanced, and took romance to new levels.

Food, schoolwork, romance, friendships, arguments, decorating, finances . . . I can't think of a time when we got it right the first time. We carpeted an entire family room in the '80s in a mint-green carpet . . . just about the time mint green had had its 15 minutes of fame. We had to live with an outdated room for the next dozen or so years. We are very careful in choosing colors now.

"SUCCESS IS STUMBLING FROM FAILURE TO FAILURE WITH NO LOSS OF ENTHUSIASM."

WINSTON CHURCHILL

Helping kids with homework was always tough. I struggled with math in school and was of no use to the kids. Algebra homework came along, and Jill and I both went nuts trying to mentor and help.

Jill finally went back to college for a couple of semesters to master algebra. The kids did fine. Jill's self-esteem soared.

Cooking, decorating, mentoring, sharing, loving, collaborating, communicating, comforting, working, learning, growing, and maturing all took time. Our marriage is still a work in progress.

Stubbornness belongs in this section too, so a few comments on being a jerk. Arguments are usually about stubbornness and rigidity. With men, it's about losing. It will take time and persistence to learn to HAVE **OPEN DISCUSSIONS, WORK THROUGH DIFFERENCES, ARGUE** THEN SETTLE, **SETTLE** THEN SETTLE DOWN AND **SETTLE DOWN** THEN SOOTHE.

Religious leader Heber J. Grant was well known for his persistence. He became famous for his penmanship, his baseball pitching, and other things. He taught, "That which we persist in doing becomes easier to do, not that the nature of the thing has changed, but our power to do so is increased."[2]

MARRIAGE IS A PERSISTENT EFFORT THAT PROGRESSES APACE TOWARD PERFECTION ONLY WITH PATIENCE AND CONSISTENCY.

OTHER THINGS P IS FOR

P *is for* Patience

Our honeymoon began on the beaches of Southern California. In the morning, I was up, in a swimsuit, and ready to head out the door. I can be ready for a day like that in less than three minutes. On day two of marriage, I discovered that it takes Jill an hour to do hair and makeup. Me: "We're going to the beach; you need to do your hair for the beach?" Her: "I want to look nice for you." Forty years later, it still takes an hour or more of prep time, and I'm still waiting and pacing. And I'm grateful she still wants to look nice for me. The Good Book says, "In your patience possess ye your souls" (Luke 21:19).

MARK HURST

P *is for . . .*

P *is for* Perseverance

My first job out of college was in the media business. I was paid $500 per month. We learned how to get by on fumes and live without a lot of fancy things. We hung in there for a year, and that job led to an offer in Washington, DC, and one of our grandest adventures. Early on we gave up a lot of things, but my persevering wife always believed in me. **PERSEVERING is the ESSENCE of PARTNERING.**

P *is for* Persuasion

Persuasion is done gently, humbly, consistently, and with dedication.

P *is for* Prevention

When I was a boy, my father took me to a remote spot in the middle of an Idaho forest, where we were given permission to climb to the top of a fire lookout station. In these stations, rangers watch for smoke, lightning strikes, human mistakes, and anything else that might pose a danger to the forest. Equipped with maps, radio gear, and other high-tech tools, the rangers can efficiently mobilize forces to extinguish any fire they see.

I was dazzled with the view and fell in love with the idea of a life spent in the forest. I contemplated becoming a forest ranger.

But the towers are all gone now. (In some states they've been converted to overnight cabins.) They don't do lookout towers any-more even though Smokey the Bear still intones, "Only you can prevent forest fires."

Think about this. We don't have watchtowers, and we don't try to prevent forest fires any more.

In 1987 and 1988, a staggering 1.4 million acres of Yellowstone National Park were ravaged by fire. A few years later, I found myself standing on its still-charred earth and spotted elements of life already making a comeback. Shoots of green were everywhere. Small plants and young lodgepole pines springing up among the dead trees—both standing and fallen—foreshadowed what would eventually take over a hundred years to re-create.

P *is for . . .*

This tragic fire started with a single lightning strike setting a small group of pines ablaze. The fire was allowed to burn under the U.S. Government's controversial natural burn policy until the fire had burned just under 50,000 acres. By then the flames were so hot that they consumed vegetation faster than even the most experienced firefighters thought possible. They lost control of it.

Eventually a total of 9,500 firefighters came from all over the country to participate in the firefighting effort at a cost of over $140 million. In the end, rain and snow put out a fire that had grown too powerful to be humanly contained or extinguished.

Because that area is a favorite vacation spot and a part of my childhood, I'm still mad about it 25 years later. I'm still smoldering. We should put the fires out.

Marriages ought to have towers and spot flames—hot spots. You know what I'm talking about. Little disagreements become major arguments at lightning speed. Rather than wait until it gets too hot to handle, and before you decide to let it burn, take time to build a tower and understand where the hot spots are.

With a watchful eye, it's possible to prevent fires that grow out of control. I think it's possible to know the source of arguments.

THE SOURCE OF ARGUMENTS ISN'T CIRCUMSTANCES OR ISSUES. IT'S YOU.

Most fights begin over stupid, idiotic, meaningless trivia. You make them big. You and your big ego and your stubbornness and your complete unwillingness to listen are the cause of fires. Again, listen to Smoky the Marriage Bear: "Remember, only you can prevent wildfires."

MARK HURST

THINGS P IS NEVER FOR

P *is* NEVER *for* Pushy

Partners don't push; they pull together.

P *is* NEVER *for* Pride

Get over yourself. You don't know anything, really. It's a marriage, for heaven's sake, not a courtroom or a football field.

> "ANY MAN MORE RIGHT THAN HIS NEIGHBOR CONSTITUTES A MAJORITY OF ONE."
>
> THOREAU

P *is* NEVER *for* Pornography

This is like heroin. It is highly addictive and the scourge of marriage; in fact, it's the scourge of a generation. It is so accessible, so affordable, and so much worse than anyone knows. Keep it out of marriage at all costs. It demeans women and detaches men. (See addendum at end of book for more information on pornography and how to get help for addiction.)

P *is* NEVER *for* Prescription

That's the thing your doctor writes for you when you are sick. Take three times daily and your problems will go away. There isn't a prescription for marriage. No rules that say if you follow this or do that, everything will work out. Like modern health care, marriage may need a new emphasis on prevention, wellness, and keeping marriage healthy. It's hard to make a marriage better with prescriptive measures. It's much easier to exercise, keep it strong, inoculate it against the pains, strains, infections, and flab of lethargy.

A

is for AUTHENTICITY

BE REAL AND BE REALISTIC. You can't be the neighbor, friend, coworker, fashion model, Hollywood starlet, or anyone or anything you think is ideal. You can't be someone else.

Now, this isn't to say that you can't change. Of course you can change! You changed dramatically when you fell in love. You changed the minute you said "I do." That promise, that covenant, really means "I will."

"I am willing, I have the will, and I'm going to try."

Of course you can change. Even Christ was not perfect at first. "Yet learned he obedience by the things he suffered" (Hebrews 5:8).

He was wise and learned as a young boy but he "gained in wisdom and in stature" (Luke 2:52). He was tried. He was tempted.

A *is for . . .*

He grew, progressed, lost his temper, and was tempted and tried and pushed and tricked and mocked.

And in the end he said, "I will."

Don't go to the altar and simply say, "I do." Say, "I will."

You can still be you and become the best you.

"HOW WOULD YOUR LIFE BE DIFFERENT IF . . . YOU APPROACHED ALL RELATIONSHIPS WITH AUTHENTICITY AND HONESTY? LET TODAY BE THE DAY . . . YOU DEDICATE YOURSELF TO BUILDING RELATIONSHIPS ON THE SOLID FOUNDATION OF TRUTH AND AUTHENTICITY."

STEVE MARABOLI

It is in lifting that we become strong. It is in bending with the wind that we put down strong roots. It is in overcoming hardship that we become wise. It is in pruning and cutting the bush that it flowers more abundantly.

Authenticity isn't about always staying the same. It *is* about staying true to values and promises. It's about saying "I do" every day—and saying "I will" all day, every day.

OTHER THINGS A IS FOR

A *is for* Abundance

Marriage is a blessing. It's not measured with money or possessions or bigger houses or bigger boats or bigger anything but with things of the heart. *Abundance* comes from the Latin word *abundantia* and means *fullness*. It was always associated with the concept of overflowing. It's a word that usually gets confused with *affluence*. I know many, many couples who are not anything close to affluent, but when I look at them, I know their marriage is abundant. It is overflowing. And I know plenty of couples who are very, very affluent, and it doesn't automatically give them abundance. Live full.

"LET OTHERS SEE THEIR OWN GREATNESS
WHEN LOOKING IN YOUR EYES."

MOLLIE MARTI

A is for…

THINGS A IS NEVER FOR

A *is* NEVER *for* Apathy

Be something. Do something. Don't let marriage wilt.

BE ***SHOCKING,***
DISRUPTIVE,
DARING,
BOLD.

DON'T ACCEPT SAMENESS. **DO** THE **UNEXPECTED** THING.

BE INVENTIVE. BE INTERESTING. **BE BRAVE.**
EXPLORE, EXAMINE, ENTERTAIN, ENTICE.

SAID ANOTHER WAY, **"GET OFF YOUR BUTT."**

A *is* NEVER *for* Arrogance

Who made you captain of the ship? You are a couple, and that word starts with *co-*. It's a prefix that means, "We're in this together, Babe." You are cocaptains. You comingle your earnings; you comingle management; you comingle parenting decisions; you comingle feelings. You are co-romantic and co-physical and co-intimate. Everything is a partnership, and you are not the boss.

A *is* NEVER *for* Abandonment

You do not walk out on a fight—you work through it. You do not walk out on tough times. You do not walk out on a marriage. And you never, never, never, never walk out on your kids.

I

is for INTEGRITY

THAT WORD MOST FREQUENTLY seems associated with ethics and the kind of thing you talk about in a corporate boardroom. We hear it a lot in business, government, finance, and education.

Is it the same as honesty? A little bit. And you can't have a good marriage without complete honesty. But integrity is something different. And within a marriage, it's *very* different.

The dictionary had two really compelling definitions for integrity. The first is what you would expect: "The quality of being honest and fair; firm adherence to a code of especially moral . . . values."[3]

"REAL INTEGRITY IS DOING THE RIGHT THING, KNOWING THAT NOBODY'S GOING TO KNOW WHETHER YOU DID IT OR NOT."

OPRAH WINFREY

But the second one caught my eye: "The state of being complete or undivided; completeness."[4]

I traveled a great deal during my career, which took me away from my family and the comfort of home. Being apart is hard. Any man or woman who travels extensively knows the temptations. There's that ever-present imp on one shoulder, traveling with you from city to city and telling you that "no one will ever know." Integrity is being real, honest, and upright, even when no one is looking. Even when your spouse isn't looking. Integrity is being who your spouse believes you are—being who you promised to be.

I love the concept of "moral uprightness." If I'm not giving advice on marriage and not telling you the rules, then I'm certainly not going to preach morality. You know what morality is, and you'll reach your own conclusions. I'm no moralist.

But I dig this concept of uprightness. It rhymes with uptightness—never a good thing in marriage—but up*right*ness is.

IT'S BEING TIGHT, **BEING STRONG,** NEVER BENDING, YIELDING, OR GIVING AN INCH **ON** THE **PROMISES** AND **CONTRACTS** AND **CONDITIONS** AND **COVENANTS** OF **MARRIAGE** **AND** **BEING** **OUTSTANDING, UPSTANDING,** AND BEING A **STAND-UP PERSON** EVEN IN THE FACE OF **TOUGH CHOICES** AND MORAL COMPROMISES

—THAT'S INTEGRITY.

Moral compromises are easy. Rationalization is simple. Marriage is tough. Be tough. Practice uprightness.

MARK HURST

OTHER THINGS I IS FOR

I *is for* Isometrics

I had a recent visit with the doctor where he and I talked about some arthritis in my spine. There's no surgery to deal with it, so we're trying to mitigate the pain. He recommended lots of muscle stretching using a term I hadn't heard in a long time: *isometrics*.

We learned about isometric contractions in junior-high gym class. I'm told this concept of muscle resistance is about pushing and pulling on the muscles without using weights. You're basically using your own body to create resistance. The famous body builder Charles Atlas was big into the concept of dynamic tension. According to these principles, you can do a lot of exercises sitting in your chair or just about anywhere.

The experts say there are two forms: **OVERCOMING and YIELDING.** This from Wikipedia: "In an overcoming isometric, the joint and muscle work against an immovable object. In contrast, in a yielding isometric, the joint and muscle are held in a static position while opposed by resistance."[5]

Explained simply, stand against a brick wall and try to push it over. You don't have the strength. But keep pushing. If you do this often enough and long enough, your muscles will lengthen and get stronger from the pressure. Yielding and Overcoming.

I believe there is a form of marriage isometrics rooted in the principles of overcoming and yielding. Marriages need exercise to prevent atrophy. To be certain, you must work to keep a marriage in shape. It can be done anywhere and anytime with isometrics. Push the bar as far as you can, then realize when there's resistance. Know when to yield and know how to overcome.

The net result is strength you didn't know you had.

I *is for* If

I had to think long and hard about this word. It can be very negative: "If only you were prettier." "If only I'd married Hank." "If only I'd listened to my mother."

In the big picture of a marriage partnership, it's easy to second guess: "If only we hadn't taken the job in Omaha."

I've chosen to make it a positive word—maybe one of the most positive words in the English language. "If I work harder, I can get a raise in salary." "If I got active in the PTA, I could ensure that my kids are getting the right curriculum." "If we will live on a budget, we can meet our financial goal and get the new couch."

Just about the time we got married, the musical group Bread recorded their most thoughtful lyrics: "If the world should stop revolving, . . . I'd spend the end with you."[6]

Even Pink Floyd sang of the ifs—and remember, they were "off the wall."

If I were a good man,
I'd talk with you
More often than I do.[7]

In the most positive sense of the word, I think **MARRIAGES should be more "iffy."**

I *is for* Insulation

In your home, insulation keeps the warm in and the cold out during the winter months. Marriages are best when kept warm. That's when sparks fly.

THINGS I IS NEVER FOR

I *is* NEVER *for* Isolation

We all need alone time and quiet time. It's important to have individual interests, friends, hobbies, and escapes. Then it's time to get back together. Isolation is about withdrawal and letting individual needs and wants dominate at the expense of the partnership.

I'm all for individuality as long as it doesn't become isolationist. In prisons, they put the worst offenders in solitary confinement. Please note I just used the word *prison*. Marriage is *not* a jail cell, but it may be possible to erect bars and create isolation zones in marriage all the same. Make sure you aren't getting locked into solitary confinement by being ornery.

I *is* NEVER *for* Iago

Iago is a character in Shakespeare's play *Othello*. He's a shady character caught up in deceit, treachery, lies, and false accusations of cheating and adultery; ultimately, he's caught up in a twisted, powerful, and destructive jealousy. *Othello* is a complicated story about an individual who doesn't get his way and does and says just about anything to aggrandize himself. There aren't many literary characters more loathsome than Iago, either on the stage, in drama, or in a real-life marriage.

> O, beware, my lord, of jealousy;
> It is the green-eyed monster which doth mock
> The meat it feeds on;
>
> IAGO, IN WILLIAM SHAKESPEARE'S *OTHELLO*, ACT 3, SCENE 3

R

is for "RE-"

THERE ARE A LOT OF *RE-* WORDS IN MARRIAGE: RENEW, REINVIGORATE, RECALCULATE, REEXAMINE, REPENT, REVITALIZE, REALIGN, REBOOT, REAWAKEN, RESET, REALIZE, REKINDLE, REIMAGINE & REINVIGORATE.

Sometimes you examine goals and reprioritize.

Renewal—many religions embrace this term. We renew promises or covenants. Christians, often weekly, set aside goofs and gaffs and glaring omissions and meet at the altar where we all can hit the reset button. We reboot, we repent, we renew promises or covenants, and we say, "I'm rededicating myself to Christ."

Marriage is built for renewal. Daily, weekly, monthly, even hourly, head up to the marriage altar and say, "Let's start over. Let's do this again. Take my hand, look me in the eye, and hear me tell you, 'I'm all in for all eternity.'"

OTHER THINGS R IS FOR

R *is for* Repentance

Step up. Be a man or woman of integrity. Be strong. Say, "I'm an idiot," "I was wrong," "I hurt you," and "I'm sorry."

R *is for* Rally

This is very close to *persistence*. Get back up and try again. In a tight game, baseball players sometimes do funny things with their caps—mostly turning them around or wearing them backwards or inside out. They call them rally caps. Every marriage should keep a rally cap, real or symbolic, handy for an emergency. When the team is down, put on a rally cap and go to work. Pull out a victory.

R *is* definitely *for* Romance

I just wish the word *lovemaking* started with an *R*. I love the concept of making love. Sex is sensational. I heard a presentation at a TED talk by a speaker who said the reason sex is so good is that it involves all five senses.[8] When I heard that, I knew it was true. Sex is good, romance is better, and making love includes movements of the heart—a combination of the senses and emotions.

MARRIAGE AND ROMANCE AND LOVEMAKING AND TENDERNESS AND TOUCHING AND TOGETHERNESS, AND LINKING AND LONGING AND LINGERING SHOULD BE A SENSORY EXPERIENCE YET NEVER EXCLUDE MOVEMENT OF THE HEART.

MARK HURST

R *is for* Reality Checks

And sanity checks. I'm really a proponent of togetherness, but, let's face it: there are times for aloneness. Go for a bike ride. Go golfing, hiking, or shopping. Go build something. If you're a woman and can't stand another minute of his noise, go, be alone, meet friends, and get creative. And vice versa.

Do the dump, drop, and dream routine:

DUMP THE **KIDS,**
DROP WHATEVER YOU'RE DOING,
WHATEVER **YOU** THINK **CAN'T WAIT,**
AND **DREAM** ABOUT ONLY YOURSELF **AND** **ALL YOU STILL WANT** TO DO.
GO AWAY AND **FOCUS** ON **YOU.**

R *is for* Realism

He's never going to make an NBA team. She is never going to make the cast of *Mama Mia!* even though she's been rehearsing those songs for ten years, and if I hear the lyrics of "Super Trooper" one more time I might just . . . wait. This is the time for that oxygen I talked about earlier. Take a breath. Reset. Relax. Let her keep on singing, and let him keep shooting hoops.

Get real. Know your limitations. Get on down the road.

Jill bought me a set of drums for my 50th birthday. When I was about 16, I was a guitarist and lead singer of the rock-and-roll band First Impression. We didn't make many first impressions—or lasting ones, for that matter. We had a grand total of two gigs, both church related. Along the way I learned to play the drums. No one ever asks you to play the drums. At a party, someone might say to a piano player, "Sit down and play us a nocturne." Even a guitar player, from time to time, can sit around the campfire and strum out a few favorite tunes. But no one ever asks you to play the drums. They are noisy, big, and at any age over 50, they cause incredible hearing loss. My drums lasted two years. My dreams of being a rock-and-roll musician went down the drain—again. But letting go of an unrealistic goal was the right thing to do. *R* may not be for *rock and roll*, but it definitely is for *realism* and *reality*.

In more modern parlance that you might hear a young person say, "Get a clue."

R *is for* Rocks

Our first home was out in the suburbs—*way* out. It was so far out that my parents stopped coming by. It was really only a 20-minute commute to town, but it seemed to aging parents that it was the end of the world.

When it came time to landscape our yard, it felt like another planet. It was actually an old farming area, and small amounts of alfalfa still popped up. But it was as rocky as the surface of the moon. Before we could plant a single blade of grass, we had to clear the rocks. It took us an entire summer to clear just the front yard. We had no tractor, no truck, and no help. One by one, we loaded rocks into a wheelbarrow with our bare hands and hauled them down to the gulley (which was probably illegal dumping that just made the rocks someone else's problem). We got strong and healthy and golden brown from a summer of lifting.

We finally got a little bit of grass planted, but it was never a great yard.

When we bought our second home and had a little more money, we put in a sprinkler system with an automatic timer. We always had a beautiful lawn.

In our third house we put in flowerbeds, trees, and other touches of semiprofessional landscaping. I became an expert on fertilizer and weed control and had a lawn that was pretty much the envy of the neighborhood. (In gardening, envy is a good thing.)

In my garden, I practiced my father's famous philosophy of "if a little bit is good, then a lot must be better." I would sometimes

R *is for . . .*

fertilize so much that I would have to mow my lawn two or three times a week, but I never complained.

After a little research, I began looking for creative ways to make our little quarter-acre lot different than all the other cookie-cutter homes lining the subdivision. I eventually had more than 120 varieties of perennial flowers and dozens of varieties of bushes, trees, fruits, and vegetables.

To some that sounds like a nightmare, but it isn't that hard to make something beautiful. It turns out that gardening isn't as difficult as it looks. Neither is marriage.

- MARRIAGE TAKES TENDER, LOVING CARE.
- GET TO THE WEEDS EARLY AND OFTEN. (Did you know they sell a preemergent product that actually prevents weeds from growing?)
- GET THE ROCKS OUT OF THE WAY. Don't be afraid of the hard work. It makes you strong.

- REGULAR NOURISHMENT KEEPS IT GREEN. If a little is good, then a lot is better.
- WITH A LITTLE EXTRA WORK AND A BIT OF CREATIVITY, YOUR MARRIAGE CAN BLOSSOM. It can become a spectacular and diverse wonderland of color, fragrance, beauty, and unexpected pleasure.
- VARIETY IS GOOD. There are hundreds of varieties of perennials to choose from. (Those are the flowers that come back year after year after year.)

THINGS R IS NEVER FOR

R *is* NEVER *for* Recalcitrant

Recalcitrant is a word we rarely use. That's because it's so much easier to say *obstinate* or *stubborn*. Typically we use it with rebellious teenagers who have bad attitudes. It sounds like *calcium*, which is a very hard substance, but the word actually comes from the Latin *calx*, which means *heels*. It means setting one's heels, digging in, and refusing to change.

Stop acting like a recalcitrant child. Lose the attitude and grow into the nature of marriage—changing yourself.

"THE THREE GREAT ESSENTIALS TO ACHIEVE ANYTHING WORTHWHILE ARE, FIRST, HARD WORK; SECOND, STICK-TO-ITIVENESS; THIRD, COMMON SENSE."

THOMAS A. EDISON

F

is for FUTURE

WHEN WE ARE YOUNG (or younger), we tend to "live in the moment." We live for fun, frivolity, excitement, and exploring. I'm great with the concept of living and staying young, and I actually love and embrace the concept of living in the moment.

But there is also a time to think about the future.

I've noticed that in my era (they call us the *boomers*), we seemed to close a generation gap just a bit. I grew up with the Beatles. To my father, who was a fan of big bands, Lawrence Welk on Saturday nights, and Mitch Miller sing-alongs, the Beatles were an atrocity. Rock and roll was "a bunch of noise" and a bunch of hair. It was obscene and obnoxious. (He certainly didn't love the world-famous band First Impression and our practice sessions in his basement.)

Later, when we got married and had kids, guess what music they grew up on? The Beatles, the Beach Boys, The Doors, The Stones, and Bob Dylan. Later we would all listen to Billy Joel and the Eagles. Then they would introduce me to Dave Matthews, Coldplay, Jason Mraz, Colbie Caillat, Adele, and others. We grew together by growing up together. There was less of a gap because we worked on closing it.

There was also less of a generation gap because we talked openly *about* gaps and how to either close them or bridge them. Jill and I came from different backgrounds—different families, approaches, opinions, and attitudes. We had to find the blueprints, build the trusses, and install the bolts that would hold our bridge together over the span.

Early on, we began talking about our kids' futures as well as our marriage goals and how they meshed with our individual and personal goals. We had financial goals as well as goals for our health and our love life. We had goals for travel, for learning, and for serving others. We had realistic notions about our dreams, and we learned how to be realistic without giving up hope.

I've never believed too much in the concept of goal setting. I realize this sounds preposterous. There's a company that makes day planners and organizers, and they are deadly serious about a system for describing and tracking daily, weekly, monthly, and even hourly goals. I suppose there are people who are that serious, but I'm not one of them. I think you can drive yourself nuts trying to micromanage time and trying to live up to your own expectations. And I'm certain you'll lose your mind trying to live up to the expectations of others.

But there is no substitute for one-on-one, person-to-person, lover-to-lover, in-depth conversations about successes and failures, expectations and hopes, plans and dreams, longings and learnings, leanings and aspirations, the mistakes you've made, the risks you're willing to take, and all the bumps in the road and potholes and walls you've hit along the way.

F *is for . . .*

The future isn't about trying to predict it or perfect it—the value in facing forward is acquiring skills to cope with everything that the unfriendly future will throw at you.

But setting goals seems like such an obvious concept. Most couples do this in one form or another even though very few are any good at tracking their progress toward their goals. It's the word *setting* that's problematic. *Setting* is a word that hints of "set in concrete," "set in stone," or "set in your ways." It means the end of a round in tennis. The sun sets at the end of the day. There's actually a negative tone about the word; it's mostly associated with endings.

SETTING. IT RHYMES WITH **FORGETTING** AND **REGRETTING** AND THOSE TWO THINGS ARE **DEFINITELY TIED TO GOALS** BECAUSE THAT'S EXACTLY WHAT HAPPENS TO MOST OF THEM.

There must be a better word. There are several candidates: *establish* goals, *reach* for your desires, *stretch* toward tomorrow, *strive* for excellence, and *push* to new heights. In fact, I'm going to suggest we throw it all out—the entire concept of goals. It's an old, tired way of thinking. Here's your new word: *reach*.

Comedian Pat Paulsen, who regularly ran for president, always ended his campaign speeches with this brilliant observation: "I can tell you without reservation that the future lies ahead."

Great marriages, too, definitely lie just ahead. *Reach*.

"I BELIEVE THAT YOU CONTROL YOUR DESTINY, THAT YOU CAN BE WHAT YOU WANT TO BE. YOU CAN ALSO STOP AND SAY, 'NO, I WON'T DO IT; I WON'T BEHAVE THIS WAY ANYMORE. I'M LONELY AND I NEED PEOPLE AROUND ME; MAYBE I HAVE TO CHANGE MY METHODS OF BEHAVING,' AND THEN YOU DO IT."

LEO BUSCAGLIA

OTHER THINGS F IS FOR

F *is for* Forgiveness

You never win an argument. Arguments only drive wedges between people. There is nothing to win in an argument. There are no prizes or trophies. You aren't appearing before the Supreme Court arguing a major case, and there are no television cameras there to stoke your ego. Have conversations about your disagreements. Make your points, get your feelings out, and maybe even blow off a little steam. Then forgive.

MOVE on.
up.
over.
ahead.

F *is for* Fidelity

"NOTHING IS MORE NOBLE, NOTHING MORE VENERABLE THAN FIDELITY. FAITHFULNESS AND TRUTH ARE THE MOST SACRED EXCELLENCES AND ENDOWMENTS OF THE HUMAN MIND."

CICERO

Treat your marriage contract as the most sacred thing you'll ever do. *Fidelity* most often means *faithful* and *true*, and that means no sexual intimacy with anyone other than your spouse. But fidelity means so much more than just being faithful to your spouse.

Think about how easy it is to be flirtatious with others outside of marriage. It's easy to be suggestive, enticing, and alluring, all without being physically unfaithful. These things can send inappropriate signals to the opposite sex, and it's possible to make a seemingly innocent emotional connection with someone without ever being physical or sexual. But it may not be so innocent. Fidelity means loyalty at every level. It means exactness. You can't have fidelity without purity, honor, and singleness of purpose.

F *is for . . .*

I grew up at a time when audio technology was coming of age, we were moving from mono to stereo technology, and the industry was all about hi-fi. In the '50s, audio manufacturers employed the phrase *high-fidelity* as a marketing term to describe records and equipment intended to provide faithful sound reproduction. High-fidelity equipment has minimal amounts of noise and distortion and an accurate frequency response. All the record albums were recorded in hi-fi. My generation turned the concept into a noun—we stopped listening to the record player and turned on the hi-fi. While marriage demands faithfulness, it must also have minimal noise and distractions. A marriage can't be distorted and must be pure and focused: one man, one woman.

"IF THEREFORE THINE EYE BE SINGLE,
THY WHOLE BODY SHALL BE FILLED WITH LIGHT."

MATTHEW 6:22

I like the term *frequency response*. A scientist may have to explain what it is, but I like it a lot. Look at that word and apply it to your marriage. I think it will mean a lot of things to you. Bottom line: **have a Hi-Fi Marriage.**

F *is for* Friendship

You always hear of someone marrying their best friend. Cicero said, "Friendship improves happiness and abates misery by the doubling of our joy and the dividing of our grief."

It may, at times, feel like it's not possible to be a parent, a companion, a quality spouse, and a good friend all at the same time. There are days when you disbelieve (SEE PERSISTENCE).

Friends are for talking with. Friends are for playing with. Friends are for getting away with and escaping from the pressures and the grind. I have a group of friends I play golf with. They are my escape. They don't have dinner with us every night, give my kids baths, help with homework, or weed the yard. That's why they're friends—they are not associated with tedium.

In a marriage, I think we need to make friendship like that. Muddle through the mundane, tackle the tedium, and then find time to be friends and engage in fun, frivolous face time—not Facebook, but real togetherness. Look deep in each other's eyes and have deep conversations. Dive deep into each other's interests and passions and concerns.

FRIENDSHIP ISN'T CHANGING MESSY DIAPERS—THAT'S **DUTY.** **FRIENDSHIP ISN'T** CLEANING DIRTY DISHES OR DIRTY TOILETS—THAT'S **RESPONSIBILITY.**

Friends take friends away from mess and duty and obligation into places of light, lightening, and enlightenment.

Be a good couple. Be a good pair. Be great lovers. Be one in your marriage. Be unified, whole, and focused. But when it comes time to be friends, go be friends.

F *is for* Fun

Lighten up. I don't know what you do for fun, but go do it. **NOW.** And do it a lot. If you don't have escapes, for heaven's sake go find some.

In our marriage, we had to exclude golf. It's my thing, my game, and my diversion. No matter how hard she tried, Jill simply couldn't hit the ball. It was more fun not to golf together.

If you don't have joint hobbies and activities, get some. When you met and dated it was all about fun, exploring, meeting a new person, and trying new things. But you did everything together.

When it was just the two of you, you went to shows, concerts, parks, pavilions, and places where you could live, love, laugh, languish, and hold each other till the sun came up.

Guess what? You still can. You might claim that you're too busy for such nonsense. **THAT** is nonsense. Get back to those moments of madness. You'll have time if you make time instead of making excuses. There is no excuse for a lack of fun in marriage.

F *is for*...

F *is for* Frivolity

Do something stupid and outrageous. Make each other laugh. Be silly. Be crazy. Be something you've never been. Do something you've never tried. Go somewhere new. Order a daring new entrée from the menu. There are lots of things you've never tried. Be frivolous for a change.

F *is for* Fighting

Not really—not if fighting is about fisticuffs or physicality. There must be zero tolerance for physical fighting. Men should never, ever, raise a hand to a woman.

Of course there are going to be disagreements. We've agreed that disagreements aren't bad if we know how to manage them, overcome them, learn from them, move on from them, and allow them to shape us.

But I have to talk about fighting. As I started collecting thoughts on marriage, I spoke with a few people about my ideas. Remarks from two women were as profound as anything I've ever heard.

I won't mention their names because they both told me about a fight they had with their husbands and the outcome of it. I don't want to embarrass either them or their husbands for these intimate yet profound moments.

The first woman, in a verbal brawl, was tearful and torn apart. Her husband, in utter frustration, said, "What do you want from me?"

Man, is that a killer question. How many times does that get asked during a fight? It's *why* we fight. We don't understand the needs/wants quotient of our spouse, and when we don't understand, we tend to ignore the situation, and when we ignore we neglect, and when we neglect we hurt, and when we hurt, we fight.

So when my friend's husband asked the big question, "What do you want from me?" my friend had a ten-year-old answer. It had been building for ten years, and she was ready.

She felt she had become an object. She felt she was largely ignored. She felt she had become a housekeeper and a janitor and a cook and that she was an employee, not a partner. She had become anything but a wife.

F *is for . . .*

HER ANSWER: "I want to be **ADORED.**"

It brought her husband to his knees. It brought them both to their knees, where they humbled themselves, turned to God, and began listening to him and to each other. They learned a lot about adoration. It's above love, above respect, and is pretty close to the top of the list of words that men should use in their relationship with women.

Women are partners with God in the creation of human life. Guys, we barely have a role in it. This makes women virtually equal to God as a creator of men—and heavenly creatures who should be adored.

WE **SHAME THEM** WHEN WE **SHUN THEM.**

WE SHAME OURSELVES WHEN WE SNUB THEM, SHUT THEM OUT, AND SELFISHLY REQUIRE THEIR SERVITUDE.

How low is a man when he treats a heavenly creature with contempt!

One fight yielded this incredible idea: women long to be adored. They *deserve* to be adored.

The second fight, which was described to me in intimate detail, yielded a similar result. The man was being recalcitrant (holy cow, I didn't think I'd be able to use that new word so soon) and a long discussion ensued. Does it matter what the details were? Usually details end up not mattering as much as the outcome.

In this case, the outcome was this:

"I just want to be **VALIDATED.**"

F *is for . . .*

This young mother has a college degree and is a bright, capable, creative woman juggling the complexities of motherhood and running a small business. Changing diapers, preparing meals, cleaning house, ironing lots of shirts, and all the dinginess and drudgery of domesticity boiled over, and she wondered if any of it mattered. Does anyone care? Does anyone notice how hard it is? Does it go on forever? What on earth have I gotten myself into?

Back to my career in advertising. When we spend billions of dollars in messaging, communications, and marketing, we always try to connect with our audience in a way that creates relevance and esteem. We want our products to have relevance in consumers' lives, and we want our customers to esteem us for the way we help them live their lives. Now, to this formula of brilliantly simple needs, I would like to add what we've learned from these two fights:

RELEVANCE, ESTEEM, VALIDATION, AND ABOVE IT ALL, ADORATION.

It took a couple of fights to get these needs out on the table. Are my female friends now getting better validation, more adoration, and more esteem? They're working on it. They're making progress. They are bridging their gaps, and they are making it happen. Their husbands now understand validation and that's a valid outcome.

E

is for EDUCATION

NEITHER MY WIFE NOR I is highly educated. We don't have a bunch of degrees on our wall. We met through friends at the University of Utah, but we weren't scholars.

Education in marriage isn't about degrees. It's about opening doors and opening minds. It's about being willing to

TAKE RISKS, CHANGE,
ADAPT, MOVE, GROW,
TAKE ADVANTAGE OF OPPORTUNITIES,
AND **IMPROVING** BY **DEGREES.**

MARK HURST

E *is for . . .*

In our quest to open doors and open minds, we will see operas we would rather have missed. We will waste time with bad movies, poorly written books, and rainy vacations. But we will also go to new places and become passionate readers. We will listen to great podcasts, sermons, lectures, and music. And then we talk about it. My wife and I rarely lack for conversation because we always want to know what the other is thinking.

> "EDUCATION IS WHAT REMAINS AFTER ONE HAS FORGOTTEN WHAT ONE HAS LEARNED IN SCHOOL."
>
> ALBERT EINSTEIN

Recently we read a book at the same time. This is possible because we downloaded it on one digital device and opened it on another. I can stay up late reading; Jill gets into bed and lasts for ten minutes. Consequently, I usually finish books before she does. One particular thriller recently raised significant ethical questions about overpopulation and the pollution of the planet. I anxiously pushed her to finish the book so we could explore both sides of the arguments. I couldn't wait to talk to her about it.

Together we have read biographies of figures as diverse as George Washington and Steve Jobs. We pour over *Lincoln* by Doris Kearns Goodwin and then marvel at the Spielberg movie version and the performance by Daniel Day Lewis. We have taken a vow against any movie with the Marvel Comics name on it; we prefer our local art house, the Broadway Theater. We'll sit through incredible foreign movies with subtitles and struggle with the European approach to symbolism long before we'll see the crassness of today's romantic comedies and the predictability of action flicks and that one-note, hackneyed snarl of Harrison Ford.

Not long ago, we set out to hike all five national parks in Utah. Along the way, we searched out local food in the most obscure places—you haven't lived until you've had grape-flavored soft-serve ice cream in Bicknell, Utah.

We've seen the Caribbean on cruise ships, all the islands of Hawaii, and virtually all of the great capitals of the world, including Moscow, Beijing, Budapest, Stockholm, Helsinki, Vienna, Geneva, Copenhagen, Bratislava, and Paris. But we've also been to more than 40 US States and virtually all of Canada; wine country in the

E *is for …*

San Francisco Bay area; the Monterey coast; and watching the sun rise on America from the top of Cadillac Mountain in Maine.

I'm not telling you that you need to travel, but you do need to explore. You don't need to spend money to be educated, but you definitely need to invest in anything that will

PRY OPEN YOUR **CRANIUM** **AND** POUR IN **NEW IDEAS, INSIGHTS,** AND INVENTIVE WAYS **OF** LIVING, LOVING, SHARING, HELPING, HOPING, ADVANCING, **ENLIGHTENING** **AND** MOVING FAR FROM THE **MUNDANE.**

“THE MORE THAT YOU READ, THE MORE THINGS YOU WILL KNOW. THE MORE THAT YOU LEARN, THE MORE PLACES YOU’LL GO.”

DR. SEUSS

E *is for . . .*

OTHER THINGS E IS FOR

E *is for* Excitement, Energy & Engagement

Do new things. Meet new people. Take a painting class and realize how ridiculously hard it is. Volunteer. Give of your time and yourself.

My stockbroker is a very good friend who, at age 55, decided to learn to play the harp. At his first recital he threw up and literally couldn't perform. He froze up. He was worse than a seven-year-old at her first piano recital. Did he every master this tricky instrument? No. Did he stretch, reach, grow, and test himself? Ask him yourself when you call him about the harp he has for sale. You can get a good harp and a good set of drums on the cheap from a couple of old guys.

Be an Energizer Bunny and just keep going and going and going. Have a marriage that is always energized.

E *is for* Earning

E is definitely not for entitlement. You are not entitled to anything in marriage. You *earn* the right to be loved. You *earn* respect.

E *is for* Encircled by Incandescent Happiness

It was Jane Austen's ideal—when Miss Elizabeth Bennet finally marries Mr. Darcy and they both overcome their glaring pride and prejudice, we feel their incandescent happiness. *E* is for *eliminating* pride and prejudice and finding incandescent happiness.

E *is for* Effervescent

Marriage is bubbly. It's a chemical reaction of love, physicality, and intimacy.

Alka-Seltzer says, "Oh what a relief it is." Have an Alka-Seltzer marriage. A little fizz cures what ails you.

E *is for …*

E *is for* Erase

It's a digital world, and it's easy to put all the harsh words, anger, resentment, sarcasm, and frustration into one digital file and hit *delete*. Don't let hard feelings hang around.

E *is for* Expectations

You can either expect the very best or you can expect moments of disappointment. Leverage Dickens and live for "great expectations."

E *is for* Edge

Jill doesn't know how to make toast. That sounds ridiculous. You put bread in the toaster, and when it pops up, it's done. Nothing to it, right? That part is fine.

What she doesn't do well is spread the jam to the edge of the bread. It's kind of like a Danish roll that you sometimes have for breakfast at a bakery or in a restaurant. They are light and flaky and very tasty, but they put a dollop of jam right in the center. You eat a bunch of bread, and then you're left with the jam.

Why not spread it to the edge?

The same holds true with mayonnaise or mustard or anything else on a sandwich. Jill insists on putting everything in the middle. It's the way she was taught, and there's no talking her out of it.

When I make toast, I spread the honey or the cinnamon or the raspberry jam all the way to the edge. In fact, I let a little bit slop over the edge. My sandwiches literally drip with dressing, and the mustard always reaches the edge. It's very messy but thoroughly satisfying.

[M]ARRIAGE should go all the way to THE EDGE

Go all in. There should be no dry, tasteless corners. Don't settle for the middle. Experiences and education should all take you to new heights and test new limits. Push limits and boundaries, and push each other to greatness. Push all the way to the edge.

MARK HURST

E *is for* Elevation

If you ever come to Utah, you'll see on our signs and our license plates the tagline "Life Elevated." I wrote that line and the brand strategy behind it. We were tasked with bringing more tourists to Utah, and it has been a phenomenal success by virtually any standard.

Everyone and their uncle Bob has stolen the line or repurposed it for their own needs. A Mexican restaurant put up a big sign promoting "Food Elevated."

So I'm sure it's OK if I rip it off. Why not?

I love the ideas of seeking higher ground and changing the way we see things by getting to an elevated place. In Utah, mountains and high places frame us and surround us.

I think we can elevate marriage. I think we can frame marriages with elevated thoughts and feelings. We can take marriage to high plateaus. Marriage should be in a constant state of lifting, climbing, and reaching for new levels of growth and togetherness.

I think we can elevate our thoughts, our conversations, and the way we treat one another. I think we can elevate romance, interactions, intimacy, and the time we spend together. We can elevate our marriages by the thoughtfulness we give to them.

MARRIAGE ELEVATED

I like it.

C

is for CONVERSATIONS

I MAKE MY LIVING in the communications industry. I am a communicator. I help companies find ways to communicate with consumers like you. I'm an expert on communications. But I want to talk about conversations.

Communications and conversations are not the same thing, though they are often thought to be the same and are easily confused. Communicating usually refers to a one-way event. Someone sends a signal, and someone else picks it up. Television and radio communicate with you.

Conversations are very different. Conversations evoke and emote and elicit responses—they're two-way communications.

Marriages should have lots of communication, and they definitely should be filled with plenty of two-way conversations, plus one additional thing:

C *is for . . .*

Marriages should be full of **CARE**VERSATIONS.

You can't truly converse while having dinner with the kids. You may be able to communicate as a family, but you can't converse as a couple.

And conversations don't count if your clothes are off. A man will tell you whatever you want to hear when you're both naked. These are not emotions or feelings; these are tactics. Men want just two things late at night: Speed and SportsCenter. Sex is a good time for sex, not a good time for conversations.

Interestingly, the word *conversation* has the same root as *opposite—converse*. It could be concluded that the word means have an argument or take an opposite point of view. The word *conversation* is Latin in origin and comes from *conversationem* or *conversatio*, meaning, "the act of living or keeping company with."

But the Latin *conversus* means *turn around*, or *opposite*, as in *conversely*.

So even though this confusing word means two completely different things, we are going to live with these definitions and be comfortable that our conversations will frequently have opposite points of view. There will be disagreements. These are things you can live with if you have meaningful dialogue about them.

"THE REASON WHY SO FEW PEOPLE ARE AGREEABLE IN CONVERSATION IS THAT EACH IS THINKING MORE ABOUT WHAT HE INTENDS TO SAY THAN WHAT OTHERS ARE SAYING."

FRANCOIS DE LA ROCHEFOCAULD

Disagreements can be agreeable when we learn to have **CARE**VERSATIONS.

Make sure they're deep careversations. Understand conversing, but never confuse it with *Converse*, as in Converse running shoes. Never run away from a serious discussion about your issues.

Careversations begin with openness, with two-way dialogue, and (men, get ready—you're going to hate this) with feelings. "Just tell me what you're feeling." "Tell me what's on your mind." And when the guys asks, "What's wrong?" the correct answer, ladies, is never, "Oh, nothing."

Our 40-year marriage began with a tactic we called the *window treatment*. There would be a disagreement or a misunderstanding, and Jill would sit in the car, stop talking, and look out the window. It is also known as the *silent treatment*, the *cold shoulder*, the *icebox*, or the *big freeze*.

Stop it. Stop it right now.

We laugh about the window treatment now, but it's still a symbol and a really good way for us to start a meaningful careversation.

Sit down, look each other in the eyes, and converse. Really, truly, deeply, honestly, openly, sincerely converse.

"A HAPPY MARRIAGE IS A LONG CONVERSATION WHICH ALWAYS SEEMS TOO SHORT."

ANDRE MAUROIS

Here's an idea, if a bit idealistic: never have a fight. Never have an argument. It is possible.

Fights are loaded with enmity, vitriol, anger, and resentment. These things have no place in a careversation. You will have disagreements, you will see a situation differently, and you won't always agree. Fine. You're two different people. It's OK to disagree. Just leave the bitterness out. Leave the accusations behind.

KNOW THE DIFFERENCE between **FIGHTING** and **FORGING,** between **ARGUING** and **AMENDING.** Learn the difference between **EXCHANGES** and **EXPLOSIONS.**

Make sure you've clarified the difference between sitting together and running away from disagreements.

SUCCESSFUL MARRIAGES MUST HAVE LOTS AND LOTS OF **CAREVERSATIONS.**

MARK HURST

OTHER THINGS C IS FOR

C *is for* caressing

Guys, SportsCenter can wait. That extra holding, touching, cuddling, canoodling, entangling, and contorting will work wonders. Did you know that both men and women produce a hormone called oxytocin? It's nickname is *the cuddle drug*. Our bodies release this powerful chemical when we cuddle, hug, have sex, touch, and show physical warmth to one another. Be touchy-feely. Be physical. Show emotions and feelings. Be demonstrative.

I'm told there are two types of men: First, the kind that can't keep his hands off a woman. Second, the kind that simply doesn't know how to be warm, physical, or expressive. I am the former. I know others who are the latter. Let me tell you something: Be hands-on. It's better to have a wife chase you out of the bedroom than to have to drag you into it.

And touching goes well beyond the bedroom. Hold hands in the movies like you used to. Hold hands in church. Sneak kisses and caresses. Hold hands often, and be touchy anywhere, anytime. Throw off a little oxytocin any old time.

Hug for no reason at all. Sneak up on her while she's cooking. Give your man a massage. Guys, I'm going to tell you straight up, you haven't lived until you've had a manicure from your wife. And a pedicure. I've done this, and I still have my manhood in place.

Get physical. Touching is touching. You never run out of oxytocin, so start making some right now.

C *is for* Children

This is a book about marriage, not about raising children. But they must be part of the conversation because they can be so dominant and demanding and draining on a marriage.

When we are married, we are told to multiply and replenish the earth. When we have children, we are partners with God in the sacred, spiritual, surreal, surprising, and shocking experience of procreating.

C *is for . . .*

The kids will have your name and they will look like you, but don't be surprised if they don't turn out like you, and especially don't be surprised if they don't turn out like you expected or wanted them to. From the time they are about three, they are individuals with their own personalities, wants, needs, attitudes, opinions, dreams, drives, demands, detours, and distractions.

Within our circle of family, friends, neighbors, and acquaintances, we have seen kids turn to bad friends, drugs, and alternate lifestyles. We are surrounded by divorce. We have several close friends and family members who had children born with disabilities, differences, and challenges that they didn't see coming.

That is the way of children. They can only be described with one word—*surprising*. (You may prefer the stronger word *shocking*.) They will surprise you with wonder and awe; they will shock you with their intelligence and their precociousness. You will be constantly surprised at how much more of the world they know than you do. And whatever surprises come your way, whatever shocking and unexpected curveballs you are thrown, children rock.

As your physical offspring, they are as much a part of you as anything. They are part of the marriage covenant, and they are part of you.

While kids will shock and surprise, they will also provide staggering and spectacular amounts of love. And no matter what curveballs they throw, love them back. Remember, we love Christ because he loved us first. Speaking of which:

C *is for* Christ

In my personal view, Christianity is about three simple things: First is love for our fellow man. Second is repentance and forgiveness. Third is taking up the cross and being willing to sacrifice and be made humble.

Striving for a Christ-centered life is our focus. Building a Christ-centered marriage is heaven.

Loving our fellow man, loving our spouse, forgiving the silly blunders we make each day, and being humble and submissive all bring us closer to Christ each day—even each hour.

"A PERSON ISN'T WHO THEY ARE DURING THE LAST CONVERSATION YOU HAD WITH THEM—THEY'RE WHO THEY'VE BEEN THROUGHOUT YOUR WHOLE RELATIONSHIP."

RAINER MARIA RILKE

C *is for* Commitment

We made a contract and a covenant the day we got married. Commitment is the extension of that. When you say you'll do something, do it right, do it well, and do it now. The contract of marriage is actually pretty easy—you stay married. But being committed to marriage takes conscious effort, focus, fever, and fervor.

C *is for* Candor

Candor is often confused with bluntness, rudeness, or brashness. Marriage should have an allowance for candor. "Does this dress make me look fat?" It's a trap, right? Candor will help a man and a woman look their best, feel their best, and be their best.

CANDOR IS RELATED TO CONFIDENCE, AND JUST A STEP OR TWO AWAY, ONE SIMPLE LETTER FROM CAN DO.

MARK HURST

C *is for . . .*

C *is for* Contentment

Sometimes, in our quest for a successful marriage, we forget to be content. If you can't figure out how to meet every single goal you set or expectation others place on you and you're going crazy trying to measure up to others, then be comfortable with contentment. Contentment doesn't mean settling. Rather, it's as simple as realizing that what you have is fantastic. Count each of your blessings.

"ENJOY YOUR ACCOMPLISHMENTS AS WELL AS YOUR PLANS."

DESIDERATA

C *is for* Congruent

Now there's a word I bet you've never heard used in a conversation about marriage. Generally it means *being in agreement or harmony*. In Geometry, it describes shapes that are identical in form.

The origins of the word *congruent* are Latin. It means *meeting together*. In fact, the Latin root *ruere* hints of *falling* or *rushing* together. Taken one step further, it may mean "hurry up and get together."

MAKE YOUR MARRIAGE ONE OF CONGRUENCY, CONSISTENCY, HARMONY, & AGREEMENT. HURRY. WHAT ARE YOU WAITING FOR?

C *is for* Cows

I spent summers up in Idaho on my grandparents' farm and learned a lot about cows. Apologies to PETA and animal lovers everywhere—these are really stupid animals. But they are also very content. Why shouldn't they be? They have a pretty sweet life. It's thought that beef and dairy products are better when they come from contented cows. I believe that. So do California cheese producers, who have convinced us that "better cheese comes from happy cows, and happy cows come from California."

C *is for . . .*

Marriages ought to strive for contentment, calmness, simplicity, and relaxation.

There's an old story about two cows grazing in a pasture. A truck pulls out of the dairy and drives past the two. The side of the truck is emblazoned with "Pasteurized, Homogenized, and Vitamin D added." One cow looks at the other and says, "Makes you feel kind of inadequate."

I learned two things about dairy cows from my days on the farm. First, they are hard to milk. The very first time you try to milk one, you grab the teat and give it a firm pull. The expert helps you understand that successful milking is a combination of a gentle squeeze, a bit of a pull, and a lot of touch. It's not easy, and it takes time to fill just one bucket.

I've never found it wise to try to be forceful in leading, loving, or cohabitating with a woman. I've discovered all the advantages of tender touch, gentle pressure, and leading but never pulling.

Dairies are now large corporations, and machines do all the milking. I wonder if the cows are as contented being hooked up to complex computerized contraptions. Lost in all of the modernization is the three-legged milking stool. It was lightweight, easy to move quickly, and its shape fit nicely under the cows' rear legs. If you haven't seen or sat on one of the things, you would assume it would lack balance. But it doesn't.

Your marriage ought to have a three-legged stool as part of the furniture. Balance in marriage is achieved when you have three things in place:

- **FRIENDSHIP.** Great friendships are built on trust, openness, honesty, and support.
- **ROMANCE.** It's like friendship, but it needs intimacy, tenderness, caring, and excitement.
- **TEAMWORK.** Teams pull together toward common goals and offer support and effort.

C *is for . . .*

I learned a lot by being a part-time farmer. It's a lifestyle filled with hard work, but I've never felt so contented.

C *is for* Climbing

I attended a business conference recently, and the theme of the event was "Climb On." It sounded like the same trite theme of growing and expanding your business that I'd heard in hundreds of business conferences before. This one, however, was different.

The head of the business organization spoke about mountaineering and a rock climbing approach called *belaying*. Teams of climbers are roped together. If one climber falls, the rest of the team is there to catch him. The person doing the catching is called the *belayer*. The speaker said there was a standard procedure for doing this. I went to Wikipedia to make sure I got this next part right. It mirrored almost perfectly what I heard from the speaker:

"Climbers should wait for a verbal confirmation from the belayer that he is ready to begin. In the US, usually the climber asks,

"ON BELAY?" or "BELAY?" and waits for the belayer to reply "BELAY ON." Once ready, the climber follows with a, "CLIMB READY" or "CLIMBING." The belayer usually acknowledges this by calling, "CLIMB ON."[9]

Marriage is a daily climb up rugged mountain peaks, and the team has to work together. I love the concept of one person hollering out, "On Belay," and the partner replying, "Belay On." And then the final decision: "Climb On."

It turned out to be one of the best business meetings I've ever attended in 40 years of suffering through these usually painful things.

But as they say on TV, "Wait, there's more!" We got through the business of the business conference, and they introduced the keynote speaker. His name was Erik Weihenmayer, and he spoke of his experience climbing Mt. Everest. He showed slides and videos, described the treachery of the Khumbu Ice Falls, and recalled traversing huge ice cracks on wobbly ladders. It was high drama on Earth's tallest mountain.

You may have never listened to a climber who summited Everest. I have a couple of times before, and it's very compelling. What made this presentation so unique? Just one tiny, simple little tidbit: Erik Weihenmayer is blind. He is the first and only blind person to accomplish this, and since then he's made it to the top of the seven tallest peaks on all the continents. And now he's learning to kayak down white water.

He has a book called *The Adversity Advantage*, and you might want to give it a read. I left the conference feeling completely deflated and elated. I felt deflated about how hard I think everything is to me, how comfortable I am sitting in my easy chair, how few times I challenge myself. Yet I left elated hearing about the tenacity and determination of someone who could have easily chosen to wallow in misery, pity, and self-doubt.

Listen to me: You have nothing to complain about. Nothing. Ever. Ever again. Your marriage has no problems. Your life has no problems. You can work everything out with an anchor to the mountain, roped together, pulling together, and reaching for the top.

Erik reached the top of the world with a good team and a lot of help. Even on the most difficult days, he continued to tell his team, "Climb on."

On days when you think marriage is tough, stop wallowing. Stop with the pity party and climb on.

T

is for TOUCH

AGAIN, THIS IS NOT ABOUT physical intimacy, although lots and lots of touching one another is highly recommended.

Touch is tenderness. Touch is being touched and moved and making magical moments. It's not the *touchy* that is confused with *testy*, as in, "My, aren't we touchy today?" or "Why are you so touchy?"

Marriage is about being in touch with your spouse's needs—knowing, sensing, and feeling that your spouse is down, discouraged, troubled, or struggling.

"TOO OFTEN WE UNDERESTIMATE THE POWER OF A TOUCH, A SMILE, A KIND WORD, A LISTENING EAR, AN HONEST COMPLIMENT, OR THE SMALLEST ACT OF CARING, ALL OF WHICH HAVE THE POTENTIAL TO TURN A LIFE AROUND."

LEO BUSCAGLIA

T *is for . . .*

The scientific explanation of touch goes like this:

> While your other four senses (sight, hearing, smell, and taste) are located in specific parts of the body, **YOUR SENSE OF TOUCH IS FOUND ALL OVER.** This is because your sense of touch originates in the bottom layer of your skin called the dermis. The dermis is filled with many tiny nerve endings [that] give you information about the things with which your body comes in contact. They do this by carrying the information to the spinal cord, which sends messages to the brain, where the feeling is registered.[10]

And that's a good way to think about the concept of touch in a marriage: It's an all-over thing. It's everywhere and everyday. It is registering feelings.

Touch is a feeling that goes straight to the brain.

There is **PHYSICAL TOUCHING:** tickling, stroking, caressing, holding, hugging, dancing, and loving.

There is **MENTAL TOUCHING,** where we stimulate thoughts, actions, respect, ideas, shared ideals, goals, dreams, and hopes. We smile together, laugh together, and create wireless connections where a raised eyebrow or a subtle grin can speak volumes.

There is **EMOTIONAL TOUCHING,** where we do things that stir the heart, like kind words, kind actions, romantic outings, forgiving, forgetting, fleeing, flying away, and getting carried away.

There is a **TOUCH OF KINDNESS.** Years ago, the phone companies invited us to "reach out and touch someone." They really wanted us to spend more money on long-distance calls (when there still was such a thing), but they knew that a simple thing like a phone call could change a day, brighten a moment, and touch a life. Small acts of kindness provide hugely touching moments.

"IT'S OFTEN JUST ENOUGH TO BE WITH SOMEONE. I DON'T NEED TO TOUCH THEM. NOT EVEN TALK. A FEELING PASSES BETWEEN YOU BOTH AND YOU ARE NOT ALONE."

MARILYN MONROE

T *is for . . .*

You can't have touch without a physical sensation—a signal to the brain.

The word *touch* comes from either the French word *touchier* or the Latin word *toccare*. Both suggest hitting or striking a bell. It's the way they used to ring the bells in the towers of churches—give them a whack.

In marriage, there is no place for the kind of touch that involves physical whacking. Violence and physical abuse is one of the great evils of our society. Men can never, ever be guilty of physical abuse, and women should never, ever have to tolerate a moment of it.

There is no hitting. But *toccare*, the Latin word, accidentally looks exactly like the phrase **TO CARE.**

What a lucky coincidence. A tender touch says to a spouse, "I care."

What a compelling new way to think about touching! Marriages should have more bell ringing. Rumor and legend have it that you know love by a first kiss and the proverbial, symbolic ringing of bells.

"EVERY HEART SINGS A SONG, INCOMPLETE, UNTIL ANOTHER HEART WHISPERS BACK. THOSE WHO WISH TO SING ALWAYS FIND A SONG. AT THE TOUCH OF A LOVER, EVERYONE BECOMES A POET."

PLATO

T *is for…*

Sound the bells often! Kiss each other morning, noon, and night. You have permission—even encouragement—to engage frequently in the art of bell ringing.

The ringing of tower bells heralded good news, celebrations, new beginnings, and homecomings. Build your home with a bell tower, and let the bells ring out all the remarkable, wildly happy moments and celebrations of marriage.

> "WHEN WE HONESTLY ASK OURSELVES WHICH PERSON IN OUR LIVES MEANS THE MOST TO US, WE OFTEN FIND THAT IT IS THOSE WHO, INSTEAD OF GIVING ADVICE, SOLUTIONS, OR CURES, HAVE CHOSEN, RATHER, TO SHARE OUR PAIN AND TOUCH OUR WOUNDS WITH A WARM AND TENDER HAND."
>
> HENRI NOUWEN

OTHER THINGS T IS FOR

T *is for* Two

It takes two to tango. One is the loneliest number. Dinner for two. Go on dates the way you used to. That doesn't mean taking the kids out for pizza. Get away. Go away. Hide away. Conspire. Collaborate. Connect. Concoct. Work **TWO**GETHER.

MARRIAGE

IS THE ART OF WORKING **TWOGETHER.**

T *is for* Truth (SEE INTEGRITY AND AUTHENTICITY ABOVE)

Never lie. Never speak or even think a lie. Be clear, be transparent, and be open. Truth sometimes has a little bit of pain that comes along with it, but not nearly as much as a broken heart that comes from a marriage built on half-truths, cheating, secrets, mysteries, and withheld information. Get it out. Get it in the open. Deal with it. There is no substitute for the trust that comes from the truth.

T *is for* Tsunami

Marriage complications will come at you in waves. As a sign in Santa Barbara indicates, there are actual tsunami zones. If you are far enough away and up on higher ground, chances are you'll never get slammed by one of these horrible events.

In marriage, don't let things overwhelm you.

You have a list of activities on your agenda, so I won't list them all, but they include scouting, soccer, sewing, and scraped knees; recitals, rehearsals, rallies, red dresses, and roast beef; parties, puppies, poopy diapers, puddles, puzzles, princesses, and parent-teacher meetings; emergency rooms, baby showers, building a doghouse and being in the doghouse; carpools, car repairs, cupcakes, and science fair projects; fights, fairs, fidgeting, and forgetting; housework, homework, home repairs, and hair cuts; balanced diets and riots, hair loss and lost keys, lost shoes, last week's leftovers, and last-minute book reports. Feeling helpless, hopeless, and overwhelmed yet? At times you will feel the towering sensation that everything and everyone is working against you, that you are alone on an island and the tsunami is coming.

Slow down. Simplify, prioritize, and focus on what matters most. Get out of the tsunami zone.

I

is for INSPIRATION

SOMEONE SAID THIS: "Life is not about the number of breaths we take but about the number of moments that take our breath away."

Year one of our marriage was exciting. We had our first daughter just about exactly on our first anniversary. (That's 12 months, for those who are counting.) We had a total of four kids by the time I was 30. There was never a dull moment.

Wait, yes, there was. There were a lot of dull moments. Did I mention that marriage is hard? We always had to go looking for inspiration. We found some in travel, music, theater, movies, romantic getaways, date nights, book groups, hiking, riding bikes, and cooking.

"ALL THE EFFORT IN THE WORLD WON'T MATTER IF YOU'RE NOT INSPIRED."

CHUCK PALAHNIUK

OTHER THINGS I IS FOR

I *is for* Illumination

Look at this simple drawing:

What do you see?

Most people will say they see the letter *L*.

Do you see the point of an arrow?

There's the corner of a box or a square.

There's two-thirds of a right triangle.

There's kind of a crooked letter *V*.

Anybody see a flagpole casting a shadow?

Now you do.

Artists see it immediately because in art and design classes students are taught to look for light sources and the shadows they cast. Artists are trained to see the world in interpretive ways. Painters know that anytime there's a light source—like the sun, for instance—there are going to be shadows that add depth and intrigue to a scene.

Here's another little test. Look at the purple-and-orange logo of a particular giant shipping company. There is something hidden in it. The story is that even the management of the company missed it at first. This is a company that ships packages because you "absolutely, positively have to have them overnight." They are fabulous at moving lots of packages very quickly, and they symbolize it with an arrow pointing forward. It's right there between the *E* and the *x*. (It's actually a lucky coincidence that occurs naturally when you put those two letters together.)

I *is for…*

Lot's of people know it's there. Many people have missed it.

In a marriage, there are lots of little things that are easy to overlook. Each of you has positive traits, values, qualities, insights, and talents that say a lot about you. They're obvious once you know that they are there. Take time to look deeply at your spouse's character traits and find the hidden gems that can move your marriage forward. They may not be as obvious as you think.

Back to the letter *L*, or the telephone pole. In a marriage, there will always be multiple ways to look at things—varying points of view on issues ranging from disciplining a child to eating healthy to balancing the checkbook. Don't be content with single points of view. Be willing to explore and listen to alternative ideas. This simple drawing also demonstrates the simple elegance and beauty of light. Marriage is a source of light and enlightenment, and is capable of lightning strikes, lightening burdens, and brightening lives.

On certain days, marriage may not be exactly what you thought it would be, but it may also be much, much more then you are seeing—and much more than you thought it could be.

I *is for* Ill

Most women are naturally good at nurturing and nursing. Most men are big babies who can't handle sickness very well. When I get a cold, it's known as a "man cold." It is bigger, badder, and so much worse than the colds other people have. It's true—right, men?

Wrong. The only truth is that most men are big babies.

But it's also true that women get sick from time to time and need nursing, comfort, a bowl of chicken soup. The marriage vow includes sickness and health—in other words, comfort and caring. Both of you, from time to time, will have to pitch in and manage messes during the down times.

Illness is a time when marriages really get tested. There are lots of bad things to clean up and air out. Physical illnesses are horrible. Little illnesses along the way need nurturing as well. These include a dented bumper on the car, a losing season for your football team, burnt roast beef, and missing out on the promotion at work. They're small things, but they make you feel bad. A good nurse

“YOU’VE GOTTA DANCE LIKE THERE’S NOBODY WATCHING, LOVE LIKE YOU’LL NEVER BE HURT, SING LIKE THERE’S NOBODY LISTENING, AND LIVE LIKE IT’S HEAVEN ON EARTH.”

WILLIAM W. PURKEY

with a tissue and a shoulder to cry on is always welcome. Sadness and disappointment count as illnesses and need the medicine of marriage, the pills of partnership, and the cure that is caring.

I *is for* Instagram

Not the highly popular social media platform. I mean the instant messages, unexpected calls, and flowers on days when a gift isn't called for.

Corny, right? Think again. Jill called me one day out of the blue. "I just called to tell you how much I love you." My response: "What's the matter? Is everything OK?" She responds, "I'm fine. I was just thinking about you and thought I'd try to make your day a little better." It did.

Women can do this. It's a fairly natural thing. Men, give it a try. You won't believe the effect an unsolicited compliment can have on a woman.

I *is for . . .*

I told you early on that I would never boast about our 40 years of marriage, but here is an exception. We got in the habit of doing these small, unexpected things for each other, and we are still doing it. It's nearly at the end of this book, but it's right at the top of my list of small things that make a huge difference in marriage. It's called *thoughtfulness*, and there is no substitute for it.

"I WAS NEVER REALLY INSANE EXCEPT UPON OCCASIONS WHEN MY HEART WAS TOUCHED."

EDGAR ALLAN POE

I *is for* Incite

Incite is the root of *incentive*. The word makes us think of inciting a riot, and that is a cool thing. Stir up your marriage—be daring and bold! Don't wait for your spouse to have a good idea for a trip, adventure, or new escapade. Be a starter, a doer, and a leader. Make sparks fly, start a fire, and burn down the boring!

"I READ ONCE THAT THE ANCIENT EGYPTIANS HAD FIFTY WORDS FOR SAND AND THE ESKIMOS HAD A HUNDRED WORDS FOR SNOW. I WISH I HAD A THOUSAND WORDS FOR LOVE, BUT ALL THAT COMES TO MIND IS THE WAY YOU MOVE AGAINST ME WHILE YOU SLEEP, AND THERE ARE NO WORDS FOR THAT."

BRIAN ANDREAS

I *is for* Immersion

Around the world, there is a very simple call to action: go all in. Get committed to your marriage—deeply committed—and immerse yourself in its success. From the very beginning, you may have to give up some things that are only about you. The word *immerse* comes from combining the Latin for *dipping into*, and the concept is one of *merging*. When we take our vows, we aren't simply saying "I do." It's more like, "I'm merging" with the one I love. Get immersed in the merger—completely, deeply immersed in marriage.

MARK HURST

I *is for . . .*

THINGS I IS NEVER FOR

I *is* NEVER *for* Insults

We've covered the topic of disagreements, cold shoulders, and all of that. When you have days where things are a little out of rhythm, be very, very careful to avoid insults. They are the most hurtful form of speech, and they are the among hardest things to take back. An insult sticks like a burr in the fur of spaniel—it doesn't come out. Hash out a problem the best you can, but never devolve into personal insults.

Saying, "I think you're wrong," or "I don't like this," or "I simply don't agree with your point of view," are all parts of an argument, a fight, or a naturally occurring disagreement. You disagree, work it out, and then move on. But the moment you say, "I can't believe this—are you stupid?" you are spewing invective, and invective pierces like a bullet and leaves a wound that's hard to heal. *Invective* comes from a Latin word meaning *abusive*, and there is no place in marriage for abuse—physical or verbal.

I is never for *invective* or *insults*.

I *is* NEVER *for* "I Told You So"

Who wants to hear that? Neither side should ever engage in being more right than the other. (See the Thoreau quote from earlier.)

I *is* NEVER *for* Idleness

The old adage is that "idleness is the devil's workshop." When a car is idling, it's at rest, going nowhere and spewing pollutants into the air.

Marriage can never be on idle. It takes two people constantly working together to have the partnership that makes progress. You might have to write down some goals (or reach for them, excuse me), practice communicating, and work on your careversations. At seven years, a marriage frequently hits its stride; at 15 years, it can become a bit mundane; and at 30 years, you start to look alike and dress alike and think alike and treat each other like furniture . . . unless. Unless you're invested in the concept of progress. We've talked a lot about illumination, education, and enlightenment, and even about inciting riots. **NOW** is a good time to get going on those things.

O

is for ONE

BECOME ONE. THAT'S EASY. Hire a preacher or go to Vegas. Getting married can be a very simple procedure. Building a marriage that lasts is quite another matter.

The word we're looking for here is UNITY. A union is about coming together. But forming a union doesn't mean we have unity.

Our country is a union of 50 very different states. We are a confederation of diverse groups coming together to form "a more perfect union." But as I write this, our government is closed, there's no budget, and there has never been a time when our country is so disunified—un-united.

Curiously, the word *unity* begins with what seems like an odd prefix: *un*-. The prefix (think "the Uncola") generally means *contrary* or *different*. How did it get attached to the concept of coming together?

Un-, as a prefix, is seen in words like *undoing*, *untying*, *undermining*, *unyielding*, and *unrelenting*. If something is hard, it may be unreasonable, unimaginable, unthinkable, or unbearable. Yet *un-* can also be part of prevention, as in *unsinkable* and *unstoppable*.

But the word *unite* stands apart from all the other *uns*. It uses exactly the same letters as *untie* (as in, "untie a knot"). We "tie the knot" when we get married, and if pulled tight, that knot can bind two ropes together or tether a ship to a dock.

MAKE SURE YOU GET THE **SPELLING RIGHT AND UNITE RATHER THAN UNTIE.**

Marriage must be about unity—being one in focus, one in goals, one in aspirations, one in dreams, and one in purpose.

Religious leader Henry Eyring speaks about the concept of hearts knitting together in unity.[11] I love the concept of knitting as related to marriage. Knitting takes separate strands of yarn and cleverly links them together to form a vast array of sweaters, scarves, socks, and other woolen wear. Marriages begin with thin threads of unlimited potential, that become intertwined, interlocked, integrated, and entangled to form families, and develop incandescent happiness.

Eyring also tells us that pride is the "enemy of unity."[12] It's good to be proud of each other, but never let pride stand in the way of unity.

Don't raise the kids separately. Have a plan for the kids and execute it together. Be united on discipline. Don't contradict each other. One wise person said of raising kids, "Have clarity, consistency, and constancy."

Embrace the concept of *#1*, as in, "You are my #1, my one and only, the only one for me." Sing out the song "One in a Million" or "Still the One."

O *is for . . .*

OTHER THINGS O IS FOR

O *is for* Observant

Do you have a junk drawer in your house? We do. You know just the drawer I'm speaking of—the one that catches everything that has not been assigned its own place. I think there must be a drawer like this in every home in America. Most of them are in the kitchen near the telephone. Ours is.

Yet there isn't a piece of junk in them. You need every item. Otherwise, you wouldn't need a junk drawer, just a garbage can. Instead, this drawer contains some or most of the following: string, rubber bands, paperclips, shirt-collar stays, buttons, safety pins, screwdrivers, screws, nails, glue, a pocket knife, picture hangers, wire, dental floss, receipts from the grocery store, coupons for Cool Whip, a few Crunch Berries, an odd assortment of broken crayons, an extension cord, an adapter to the cell phone charger, several of those hooks for hanging drapes, ticket stubs, unused gift cards,

“WE ARE ONE, AFTER ALL, YOU AND I; TOGETHER WE SUFFER, TOGETHER EXIST AND FOREVER WILL RECREATE ONE ANOTHER.”

PIERRE TEILHARD DE CHARDIN

O *is for . . .*

Legos, pencils with broken lead, pens that rarely work, and a pair of scissors.

Go check your junk drawer. You have one, and I bet you have most of the same things in yours. If so, it's probably so heavy that it's hard to open and the bottom keeps falling out. Or it jams a lot because something—like that pair of scissors—keeps sticking up high enough to catch the lip of the cabinet.

Yep, they are all the same, and they hold everything you need. That is, if you can find what you're looking for. I can never find the scissors. They're invisible. No, that isn't exactly true. Jill can find them in an instant. I guess it's a malfunction in my brain. When I look in the junk drawer, all I see is junk—all of it and all at once. I can't distinguish between the Crunch Berries and the crayons. It's just junk.

"Where are the scissors?" I yell. "Why can't I find the scissors?"

"They're in the junk drawer," my wife patiently says.

"Well, *of course* they're in the junk drawer. I'm *looking* in the junk drawer."

Knowing all about my brain's malfunction, Jill comes to the rescue and, without looking, snatches the scissors out of the drawer with the pinpoint accuracy of a laser-guided smart bomb launched from an unmanned drone.

"Where were those? Why couldn't I see them?"

"Because," she answers with the wisdom of Solomon and the bite of a bulldog, "you weren't looking."

I glare at her, grab the scissors, and sulk away to do my cutting. She just did hers.

I try to stay away from that junk drawer now. I don't put anything in it, and I don't take anything out. Perhaps that's not the mature way to deal with my problem, but it makes me feel better.

The trouble is, this quirk manifests itself elsewhere. Don't send me to a hardware store. I can't spot the nails from the gardening tools. Also, don't send me to the grocery store to get cake mix. I'll come back with dill pickles and a box of Crunch Berries like the ones I saw in the drawer.

O *is for . . .*

I'm not certain marriages can tolerate a junk drawer—a place to catch stuff that's old and maybe rusty. But I think we can learn a lot from the lessons of the junk drawer. You need to know where to look, how to look, and how to focus without getting distracted. You need to take the time to be observant about the strengths you each have, your grand ideas, insights, intelligence, tenderness, and the touch that made you fall in love.

It's all there if you just know where to look.

> "I'M SELFISH, IMPATIENT, AND A LITTLE INSECURE. I MAKE MISTAKES, I AM OUT OF CONTROL, AND AT TIMES HARD TO HANDLE. BUT IF YOU CAN'T HANDLE ME AT MY WORST, THEN YOU SURE AS HELL DON'T DESERVE ME AT MY BEST."
>
> MARILYN MONROE

O *is for* Ohhh's

And OOOOH's. And AHHHH's. When you met and were first attracted to each other, there were lots and lots of these feelings and expressions. When you first put that engagement ring on, there was a big OOOOOHHH. Moments of gift giving, intimacy, instagrams (again, not the social media platform), and other things can still produce feelings of pure pleasure.

Guys, let me ask you something. After a few years of marriage, you've settled into a comfort zone. On the rare occasion that you hold the door or help her with her coat, does she say, "Oh?" (Meaning, "Oh, I didn't think you did that anymore.") Or does she still say, "OOOOOHHH," meaning, "You're so thoughtful and considerate, and you continue to treat me like a woman"?

I realize this is old school. Right? Wrong. If you think these small things can't elicit an OOOHH, then you are an idiot. Wait, calling you an idiot would be an insult, and that's no way to win an argument. (SEE THE SECOND CHAPTER "I") Little things still matter in a marriage, and they still have lots of OOOHH power to them.

"IT IS NOT A LACK OF LOVE, BUT A LACK OF FRIENDSHIP THAT MAKES UNHAPPY MARRIAGES."

FRIEDRICH NIETZSCHE

N

is for NOTHING and NO ONE

NOTHING SHOULD STAND between the two of you, and no one should be a better friend to you than your spouse.

You should never have to say, "I've got your back," because you should always be standing side by side, arms linked—unified. I might stand behind her decisions, but I'm always going to be in the front of her mind. And I'm going to be in front of her, leading the way, fighting for her, blazing trails we can both walk and making sure no bad guys, bears, bullies, or bogeymen ever get near.

When she needs a shoulder to cry on, it should never be her girlfriend's or her mother's. When a guy needs to vent, it should never be to his best buddy or his golf partner. They should talk to each other. Talk it out. Work it out. Walk it off. Sit down, listen, learn, and lean in for support.

There is nothing worth fighting about, and there is no one more worth standing up for than the love of your life.

OTHER THINGS N IS FOR

N *is for* Near

Close to my heart. At my side.

The song "The Nearness of You" is a golden oldie from another generation recently made profoundly modern by Norah Jones:

> It's not the pale moon that excites me
> That thrills and delights me . . .
> It's just the nearness of you.[13]

It was written a long time ago but has never had more relevance. Turn down the lights, pull down the sheets, put on some Norah Jones, and nothing else matters.

"My Romance" is another deeply meaningful song. Rodgers and Hart wrote:

> My romance doesn't need a castle rising in Spain
> Or a dance to a constantly surprising refrain . . .
> My romance doesn't need one thing but you.[14]

N *is for*…

N *is for* Nirvana

Nirvana is supposed to be the ultimate existence—a transcendant state of happiness and contentment. Now, we've all agreed that marriage isn't always pretty or perfect or transcendent. But when you think about living without the friendship and companionship and the intimacy of your lover and friend, you'll realize you are much, much closer to nirvana than you think.

N *is for* kNowing

I know the spelling is wrong, but it has the right sound. Marriage is about knowing each other's wants, needs, habits, secrets, thoughts, longings, dreams, fears, and weird and quirky qualities . . . and being there to always love one another despite the quirks.

N *is for* Nighttime

Go to bed together. It's the best time to bond. Cold sheets, cold feet, spooning, and the joint BTUs that come from being together under the covers have no substitutes. No movie or football game is more important than the quiet time of nighttime and a couple wrapping up the day by wrapping up in each other's arms.

This may not be for everyone. I realize that. I know a couple who never goes to bed at the same time. The husband crashes early because he travels a lot. The wife stays up and vacuums. She is very committed to being tidy, and late nights are a good time for her. (And she's a freak about vacuuming.)

Some people don't sleep very well and are night owls. I get it. There is no single prescription for going to bed together all the time. But it's a concept, a theory, and a good idea to devote end of day to each other. Clear off all the other debris, detritus, dust, and damage of the day and get together.

N *is for . . .*

THINGS N IS NEVER FOR

N *is* NEVER *for* Negative

Find the good in each other at least once a day. Remind each other of the good things. Focus on things that matter, not the pesky, trivial, meaningless, and mundane. Stay positive, upbeat, and optimistic till, as Billy Joel said, "that old second wind comes along."

N *is* NEVER *for* Never

I know an extremely wealthy couple who didn't have a couch in their house for the first 20 years of marriage. Instead, they used an old church pew. It was all they needed while they amassed their fortune. They have lots of couches now.

You can't have a big home furnished with luxuries right away. You can't have fancy cars and toys if you have to go into debt for them. You can't take a lot of vacations—yet. Your kids can't go to private school. But you won't always be poor. Good things come with hard work and patience, so stop crying and feeling like nothing good is ever going to come your way.

Have lots of dreams and ambitions. Expect that great things will happen, attack your dreams with alacrity, and you'll get there. (Just in case you don't know what *alacrity* means, it's another word for "cheerful readiness.")

SUMMARY

I'M GOING TO END THIS BOOK by repeating the very last sentence of the very last chapter. It was pure coincidence that it was at the very end, but I think it's a good final word, thought, and action:

ATTACK MARRIAGE WITH ALACRITY

Attack doesn't have to be negative concept. In fact, it's a very positive concept. It reminds us that marriage, under the best of circumstances, takes vigilance and constant hard work. When we do it with "cheerful readiness," it produces startling results.

SUMMARY

"IF EVER THERE IS TOMORROW WHEN WE'RE NOT TOGETHER, THERE IS SOMETHING YOU MUST ALWAYS REMEMBER. YOU ARE BRAVER THAN YOU BELIEVE, STRONGER THAN YOU SEEM, AND SMARTER THAN YOU THINK. BUT THE MOST IMPORTANT THING IS, EVEN IF WE'RE APART . . . I'LL ALWAYS BE WITH YOU."

WINNIE THE POOH

I hope you've found a nugget or two in here to help you think about your marriage and what it means to you. You'll find good solutions on your own, and you don't need me or anyone else telling you what to do. So let's leave it with the notion that whatever your approach, whatever means you devise to make your marriage work, to make it strong and make it lasting, remember one final advertising slogan:

MARRIAGE: It brings good things to LIFE.

(Sorry GE)

REFERENCES

1. *Teachings of Presidents of the Church: Lorenzo Snow* (Salt Lake City: The Church of Jesus Christ of Latter-day Saints, 2012), 198.
2. Heber J. Grant, *Gospel Standards*, comp. G. Homer Durham (1941), 355 (The quote is sometimes attributed to Ralph Waldo Emerson)
3. *Merriam-Webster Online Dictionary*, s.v. "integrity," accessed May 15, 2014, www.merriam-webster.com/dictionary/integrity
4. Ibid.
5. Wikipedia, s.v. "Isometric Exercise," accessed May 16, 2014, http://en.wikipedia.org/wiki/Isometric_exercise.
6. Bread, "If," on *Manna*, Elektra, 1971.
7. Pink Floyd, "If," on *Atom Heart Mother*, Harvest and EMI Records, 1970.
8. Jinsop Lee, "Design for All 5 Senses," February 2013, TED Talks, https://www.ted.com/talks/jinsop_lee_design_for_all_5_senses.
9. Wikipedia, s.v. "Belaying," accessed May 16, 2014, http://en.wikipedia.org/wiki/Belay.
10. The Oracle Education Foundation, "Your Sense of Touch," http://hes.ucfsd.org/gclaypo/senses/download/touch.ww/thinkquesttouch.html, accessed May 16, 2014.
11. Henry B. Eyring, "Our Hearts Knit as One," *Ensign*, November 2008, 68–71.
12. Ibid., 70.
13. Norah Jones, cover of "The Nearness of You" by Hoagy Carmichael and Ned Washington, on *Come Away with Me*, Blue Note Records, 2002.
14. Richard Rodgers and Lorenz Hart, "My Romance," from *Jumbo*, 1935.

MARK HURST was born to be an ad guy. To this day he can sing lyrics to jingles from the '50s and '60s. He was grounded and influenced by what his mother (and pretty much every Idaho mother in the '60s) would call a TV addiction. After studying communications at the University of Utah, he spent the next 35 years of his life telling stories on TV, mostly in the form of thirty- and sixty-second commercials. He spent half of his career writing clever headlines, catchy jingles, and snappy taglines and the other half convincing people that there was more to advertising than clever headlines, catchy jingles, and snappy taglines. Now, as a nationally respected strategic brand strategist, he is authoring a book on that subject and has written half a dozen children's books for his thirteen grandchildren. Hurst lives in Holladay, Utah, where he serves as the CEO of Connect Partners, a venture capitalist firm. He has been married to his wife, Jill, for 40 years, a milestone that prompted him to write *Pairfection*. They have four children.

I WAS PROMPTED TO WRITE THIS BOOK as a result of seeing many marriages struggle and fall apart. One of the most serious issues of this generation is the damage to marriages from the use of pornography. Pornography is highly addicting and condemns the addict to a life of isolation and withdrawal.

I am not going to keep any of the profits from the sale of this book. Rather, I'll be giving it to an organization that helps pornography addicts deal with their challenges by reestablishing personal relationships. You can learn more about this by visiting their website, www.Candeocan.com.

0 26575 14801 5